9-3-57

WINGS OF THE FOREST

By Dr. William J. Long

WINGS OF THE FOREST
THE SPIRIT OF THE WILD

Wings of the Forest

by

DR. WILLIAM J. LONG

Drawings by Ray Houlihan

DOUBLEDAY & COMPANY, INC., GARDEN CITY, N.Y., 1957

995582

Contents

Ch'geegee-Lokh-Sis

THAT is the name which the northern Indians give to the black-capped titmouse, or chickadee. It means "Little Friend Ch'geegee," for the Indians, like everybody else, are fond of this cheery little brightener of the northern woods. The first time I asked Simmo, my Indian guide, what his people called the bird, he answered with a smile. Since then I have asked other Indians, and always a pleased look lit up their dark grim faces as they told me. It is another tribute to the bright little bird's influence.

Chickadee wears well. He is not in the least a creature of moods. Step out of the door some bright morning, and there he is among the shrubs, flitting from twig to twig; now hanging head down from the very tip to look into a terminal bud; now winding upward about a branch, peering industriously into every crevice. An insect must hide well to escape those bright eyes. Chickadee is helping you raise your plants. He looks up brightly as you approach, hops fearlessly down, and looks at you with frank, innocent eyes. *Chick a dee dee dee dee! Tsic a dee-e-e?*—the last with a rising inflection, as if he were asking how you were, after he had said good morning. Then he turns to his insect hunting again; he never wastes more than a moment talking. But he twitters sociably as he works.

It is the same in the depths of the wilderness. The smoke of the campfire has hardly risen to the spruce tops, when close beside you sounds the same cheerful greeting and inquiry for your health. There he is on the birch twig, bright and happy and fearless! He comes down by the fire to see if anything has boiled over, which he may dispose of. He gratefully picks up the crumbs you scatter at your feet. He trusts you; he rests a moment on the finger you extend, looks curiously at the nail, and sounds it with his bill to see if it shelters any harmful insect. Then he goes back to his birch twigs.

On summer days he never overflows with the rollicksomeness of the bobolink and oriole, but takes his abundance in quiet contentment. I suspect it is because he works harder in the winter and his enjoyment is deeper than that of others. When the snow lies deep, he is the life of the forest. He calls from the edges of the bleak caribou barrens, and his greeting somehow suggests the May. He comes into your rude bark camp, and eats of your simple fare, and leaves a bit of sunshine behind him. He goes with you, as you force your way heavily through the fir thickets on snowshoes. He is hungry, perhaps, like you, but his note is none the less cheery and hopeful.

When the sun shines hot in August, he finds you lying under the alders, with the lake breeze in your face, and he opens his eyes wide and says: "*Tsic a dee-e-e?* I saw you last winter. Those were hard times. But it's good to be here now." And when the rain pours down, and the woods are drenched, and camp life seems altogether beastly, he appears suddenly with a greeting as cheery as the sunshine. His cheerfulness is contagious. Your thoughts are better than before he came.

Really he is a wonderful little fellow; there is no end to the good he does. Again and again I have seen a man grow better tempered or more cheerful, without knowing why he did so, just because Chickadee stopped a moment to be cheery and sociable. I remember once when a party of four made camp after a driving rainstorm. Everybody was wet; everything soaking. A lazy man had upset a canoe, and all the dry clothes and blankets had just been fished out of the river. Now the lazy man stood before the fire, looking after his own comfort. The other three worked like beavers, making camp. They were in ill humor, cold, wet, hungry, irritated. They said nothing.

A flock of chickadees came down with sunny greetings, fearless, trustful, never obtrusive. They looked innocently into human faces and pretended that they did not see the irritation there. "*Tsic a dee.* I wish I could help. Perhaps I can. *Tsic a dee-e-e?*"—with that gentle, sweetly insinuating up-slide at the end. Somebody spoke, for the first time in half an hour, and it was not a growl. Presently somebody whistled—a small little whistle—but the tide had turned. Then somebody laughed. "I believe those chickadees make me feel good-natured," he said, hanging up his wet clothes before the fire. "Seem kind of cheery, you know, and the crowd needed it." But Ch'geegee, picking up his cracker crumbs, did not act at all as if he had done the most to make camp comfortable.

There is another way in which he helps, a more material way. Millions of destructive insects live and multiply in the buds and tender bark of trees. Other birds never see them; but Chickadee and his relations leave not a twig unexplored. His bright eyes find the tiny eggs hidden in the buds; his keen ears hear the larvae feeding under the bark, and a blow of his bill uncovers them in their mischief-making. His services of this kind, though rarely acknowledged, are enormous.

Such a bright, helpful little fellow never should have an enemy in the world; and I think he has to contend with fewer than most birds. The shrike is his worst fear; the swift swoop of his cruel beak is always fatal in a flock of chickadees. Fortunately the shrike is rare with us; one seldom finds his nest, with poor Ch'geegee impaled on a sharp thorn nearby, surrounded by a varied lot of ugly beetles. The owl sometimes hunts Chickadee at night; but he sleeps in the thick pine shrubs, close up against a branch, with the pine needles all about him, making it very dark; and with the darkness and the needles to stick in his eyes, the owl generally gives up the search and hunts in more open woods.

Occasionally the hawks try to catch him, but it takes a very quick and a very small pair of wings to follow Chickadee. Once in the winter I was watching him hanging, head down, from an oak twig to which the dead leaves were clinging. Suddenly there was a rush of air, a flash of mottled wings and fierce yellow eyes and cruel claws. Chickadee whisked out of sight under a leaf. The hawk passed on, brushing his pinions. A brown feather floated down among the oak leaves. Then Chickadee was hanging, head down, just as he was before. "*Tsic a dee?* Didn't I fool him!*" he seemed to say. He had just gone around his twig, under a leaf, and back again; the danger was over. When a hawk misses like that he never strikes again.

Boys generally have a kind of sympathetic liking for Chickadee. They may be cruel or thoughtless to other birds, but seldom so to him. He seems somehow like themselves.

Two barefoot boys were hunting with bows and arrows, one September day, about the half-grown thickets of an old pasture. The older one was teaching the younger how to shoot. A robin, a red squirrel, and two or three sparrows were stowed away in their jacket pockets; a brown rabbit hung from the older boy's shoulder. Suddenly the younger raised his bow and drew the arrow back to its head. Just in front a chickadee hung and twittered among the birch twigs. But the older boy seized his arm.

"Don't shoot—don't shoot him!" he said.

"But why not?"

"'Cause you mustn't—you must never kill a chickadee."

And the younger, influenced more by a certain mysterious shake of the head than by the words, slacked his bow cheerfully; with a last wide-eyed look at the little gray bird that twittered and swung so fearlessly near them, the two boys went on with their hunting.

No one ever taught the older boy to discriminate between a chickadee and other birds; no one else ever instructed the younger. Yet somehow both felt, and still feel after many years, that there is a difference. It is always so with boys. They are friends of whatever trusts them and is fearless. Chickadee's own personality, his cheery ways and trustful nature had taught them, and among all the boys of that neighborhood there is still a law, of which no man knows the origin: *Never kill a chickadee.*

If you ask the boy there, "Why not a chickadee as well as a

sparrow?" he shakes his head as of yore, and answers dogmatically: " 'Cause you mustn't."

If you meet Chickadee in May and he seems preoccupied or absorbed, you may know that he is building a nest or that he has a wife and children nearby. If you know him well, you may even feel hurt that Little Friend Ch'geegee, who shared your camp and fed from your dish last winter, should this spring seem just as frank, yet never invite you to his camp; in fact, he might even head you away from it. But the soft little nest in the old knothole is the one secret of Chickadee's life; and the little deceptions by which he tries to keep it are at times so childlike, so transparent, that they are even more interesting than his frankness.

Chickadee's nest is always neat and comfortable, just like himself. It is a rare treat to find it. He selects an old knothole, generally on the sheltered side of a dry limb, and chisels a deep tunnel through the heart of it. In the dry wood at the bottom he makes a little round pocket and lines it with the very softest material. A nest like this with five or six white eggs delicately touched with pink, and a pair of chickadees gliding about it, half fearful, half trustful, is altogether such a beautiful little spot that I cannot believe anyone would be mean enough to disturb it.

One thing about the nests has always puzzled me. The lining generally is made with some rabbit fur. Sometimes, indeed, there is nothing else, and a softer nest one could not wish to see. But where does Chickadee get the fur? He would not, I am sure, pull it out of Br'er Rabbit, as the crow sometimes pulls wool from the sheep's backs. Are his eyes bright enough to find it, hair by hair, where the wind has blown it down among the leaves? If so, it must be slow work, but Chickadee is very patient. Sometimes in spring you may surprise him on the ground, where he never goes for food, and at such times he is always shy. He flits up among the birch twigs, and twitters and goes through an astonishing gymnastic performance to hold your attention and make you forget that you caught him fur hunting, and near his nest.

One afternoon in May I was prowling about an old deserted farm in the hills. It was one of those sunny places that the birds love, because some sense of the human beings who once lived there still clings to the half-wild fields and gives protection. The birds were everywhere, flashing out of the pine thickets into the birches in all the joyfulness of nest building, and filling the air with life and melody.

I sat down at the edge of a pine thicket and became as much as possible a part of the old stump which was my seat. In front of me an old rail fence wandered across the deserted pasture, struggling against the blackberry vines which grew profusely about it and seemed to tug at the lower rails to pull them down to ruin. On either side the fence disappeared into thickets of birch and oak and pitch pine, planted, as were the blackberry vines, by birds that stopped to rest a moment on the old rails. Here and there a leaning post was overgrown with woodbine. The rails were gray and moss-grown. Nature was trying hard to make it a bit of the landscape; it could not much longer retain its individuality. The wild things of the woods had long accepted it as theirs.

As I sat there, a robin hurled himself upon the fence from the top of a cedar, where he had been a moment before, practicing his mating song. He did not intend to light, but some idle curiosity, like my own, made him pause a moment on the old gray rail. Then a woodpecker lit on the side of a post and sounded it softly. But he was too near the ground, too near his enemies to make a noise; he flew to a higher perch and beat a tattoo that made the woods ring. He was safe there, so he could make as much noise as he pleased. A wood mouse stirred the vines and appeared for an instant on the lower rail, then disappeared as if very much frightened at having shown himself in the sunlight.

Presently a red squirrel rushed out of the thicket at the left, scurried along the rails and up and down the posts. He went like a little red whirlwind, although he had nothing whatever to hurry about. Just opposite my stump he stopped his rush with marvelous suddenness; chattered, barked, scolded, tried to make me move; then he went on and out of sight at the same breakneck rush. A jay stopped a moment in a young hickory above the fence to whistle his curiosity, just as if he had not seen it fifty times before.

I was weaving an idle history when a chickadee twittered in the pine behind me. As I turned, he flew over me and lit on the topmost mossy rail. He had something in his beak; so I watched to find his nest, for I wanted very much to see him at work. Chickadee had never seemed afraid of me, and I thought he would trust me now. But he did not. He would not go near his nest. Instead he began hopping about the old rail, and pretended to be very busy hunting for insects.

Presently his mate appeared, and with a sharp note he called her down beside him. Then both birds hopped and twittered about the rail, with apparently never a care in the world. The male especially seemed just in the mood for a frolic. He ran up and down the mossy rail; he whirled about it until he looked like a little gray pinwheel; he hung head down by his toes, dropped and turned like a cat, so to light on his feet on the rail below. While watching his performance, I hardly noticed that his mate had gone until she reappeared suddenly beside him. Then he disappeared, while she kept up the performance on the rail, with more of a twitter and less of the gymnastics. In a few moments both birds were together again and flew into the pines out of sight.

I had almost forgotten them in watching other birds, when they reappeared on the rail and went through a similar performance. This was unusual; and I sat very quietly, very much interested, although a bit puzzled, and a little disappointed that they had not gone to their nest. Both times they had had some material in their beaks and were now probably hunting for more. But what had they done with it? Perhaps they had dropped it to deceive me. Chickadee does that sometimes. But why did one bird stay on the rail?

I left my stump and began to examine the posts of the old fence carefully. Chickadee's nest was there somewhere. In the second post on the left I found it, a tiny knothole which Chickadee had hollowed out deep and lined with rabbit fur. It was well hidden by the vines that almost covered the old post, and gray moss grew all about the entrance. A prettier nest I had never found.

I went back to the pines and sat where I could just see Ch'geegee's doorway. No other birds interested me now. The chickadees were soon back, hopping about on the rail as before, with just a wee note of surprise in their soft twitter at my changed position. This time I was not to be deceived by a gymnastic performance, however interesting. I kept my eyes fastened on the nest. The male was going through his most difficult feats, doing his best to engage my attention, when I saw his mate glide suddenly from behind the post and disappear into her doorway. I could scarcely be sure it was a bird. It seemed rather as if the wind had stirred a little bundle of gray moss. Had she moved slowly I might not have seen her, so closely did her soft gray cloak blend with the weather-beaten wood and moss.

In a few moments she reappeared, waited a moment with her tiny head peeking out of the knothole, then she flashed around the post out of sight; and when I saw her again it was as she reappeared suddenly beside the male.

Then I watched him. While his mate whisked about the top rail he dropped to the middle one, hopped gradually to one side, then dropped suddenly to the lowest one, half hidden by vines, and disappeared. I turned my eyes to the nest. In a moment there he was—just a little gray flash, appearing for an instant from behind the post, only to disappear into the dark entrance. When he came out again I had but a glimpse of him until he appeared on the rail near me, beside his mate.

Their little ruse was now quite evident. They had come back from gathering rabbit fur and found me, unexpectedly, near their nest. Instead of making a fuss and betraying it, as other birds might do, they lit on the rail before me and were as sociable as only chickadees know how to be. While one entertained me and kept my attention, the other dropped to the bottom rail and stole along behind it; then up behind the post that held their nest, and back the same way after leaving his material. Then he held my attention while his mate did the same thing.

For two hours or more I sat there beside the pine thicket, while the chickadees came and went. Sometimes they approached the nest from the other side, and I got only a glimpse as they glided into their doorway. Whenever they approached from my side they always stopped on the rail and went through their little performance to distract my attention. Gradually they grew more confident, reassured by my stillness; or perhaps they thought they had entertained me so well I did not even suspect them of nest building.

As the afternoon wore away and the sun dropped into the pine tops, the chickadees grew hungry and stopped their work. They were twittering among the young birch buds when I left them, sharing their best finds generously and calling softly to each other lest they stray too far apart while hunting their supper.

Teedeeuk, the Blue Jay

MY earliest impression of Teedeeuk was that he gave life and color and a voice to the winter landscape which without him would be a frozen silence. And to this day there is something in the bright flash of his wing or his rousing call that heartens a lone man in the solitude like the first gleam and crackle of a campfire. Not until he has gone away to his own mysterious affairs does one ask, with a vague wonder: What fickle character is hidden under his gay feathers? What merry or mocking spirit animates him when he swoops silently at a cat, or whistles at a man, or sounds his tallyho over a hunted fox, or sends back the wild cry of a circling hawk?

Since these questions are beyond me or any man, my purpose is to let Teedeeuk himself answer them by his action. Even so he may easily be misunderstood because, more than any other bird of my acquaintance, he has a way with him, a way which changes to suit whatever part he may be playing in the wood folk comedy. Thus, he looks like a gallant when he flits in haste to answer a distress call, his crest cocked like a champion; or he seems ingratiating when he finds me quiet in the woods and perches near my head to repeat his Indian name.

His name is like other bird sounds in that it has different meanings when uttered on a higher or lower pitch, in *forte* or *pianissimo* volume. The last two syllables of that name, with the *dee* prolonged and accented, are the blue jay's alarm call as he speeds over pasture and woodland. There was a time, long ago, when it sounded like a cry of "thief, thief," which amused me the more because he himself was a thief from my small human viewpoint. In the glad autumn days, jays and squirrels store up food against a time of need, and either is ready to snitch whatever he finds in the other's storehouse. Once, to my delight, when Meeko, the red squirrel, caught a blue jay stealing some corn he had hidden he flew into a violent rage, calling down the wrath of squirrel heaven on all the tribe of jays. And it seemed to me that Teedeeuk's voice had a sound of derision as he flew away, trailing behind him as many yells of "thief, thief, thief" as there were knots in the tail of my home-made kite.

The first time his Indian name ever sounded softly in my ear with a new meaning was on a winter day when I found a blue jay caught in a jump trap, which a neighbor's boy had sprinkled liberally with grain and set under a cedar. In pecking at the bait Teedeeuk had sprung the trap, which clamped on the base of his bill, holding him fast but harming him not at all. There was no fear in his bright eye when I bent over him, but only bewilderment, and something else that may have been surprise or relief at my coming. When set free he obeyed his first impulse by flying off with a cry of resentment; but in a moment he returned, apparently forgetful of the trap in his curiosity over the boy. From branch to branch of the cedar he flitted, just out of reach, repeating his Indian name with variations, *dee-uk, tee-dee-uk, tiddy-dee-uk*, each with an up-slide, as if saying in his most charming way, "You might at least tell me who you are, and what you are doing here, and where your nest is."

How could a boy confidently interpret the anima of a blue jay? The answer is simple. Aside from action, which is at times the only guide to the mentality of birds or animals, Teedeeuk always gives one visible sign of his changing emotions. Even as we may know something of the mind of a dog from his tail, whether it is stiffened or waving or wagging, so we may enter into the mind of a blue jay by keeping an attentive eye on his crest, which is seldom quiet except when he is himself at rest. When well pleased with what he sees or hears or does his crest is straight up and down, and all its feathers are as one feather. When he is greatly surprised or excited the crest points forward of the perpendicular, or if he is frightened it bristles out like a bottle brush. When he is puzzled the crest rises and falls, constantly changing both size and shape. If he steals away like a wisp of smoke to find out where a vixen makes a den or a squirrel hides sweet acorns, then all his feathers are snugged down so close that he seems to have no crest at the very moment when it is eloquently telling what Teedeeuk does not want to be noticed—that he is snooping into what the wood folk might regard as their private affairs.

This last habit is a possible explanation of why some birds

show uneasiness or hostility when a blue jay appears among them at a winter feeding table. And the explanation is, in a word, that they dislike to be watched. All natural creatures are disturbed to find a stranger keeping tabs on them, which Teedeeuk often does. It is his particular pleasure to play the role of Paul Pry, as we shall see, and although he does no harm by his prying it may be that wood folk have the same aversion to such a character as we feel when he appears in human form.

It is said that the blue jay is a cruel bird, a troublemaker, a nest robber, a killer of fledglings, a feathered villain, and a reprobate. Some small part of this indictment may be true, although it sounds like a variation of the same judgment. One should, I think, be a bit more careful about bearing false witness against a bird neighbor.

Now it happens that in my childhood, when birds of all kinds were more abundant than they are now, one of my winter pleasures was to watch the many-feathered folk that flocked to the table I set for them. I knew less than half their names and only so much of their dispositions as they revealed by their action. Child training was rather strict in those days, when good manners were the hallmark of good breeding, and it seemed to me that Teedeeuk had excellent table manners. For all his bold appearance he was, next to the lovable chickadees, the most careful to give no offense, and what I then called his politeness stood out in contrast with the rudeness of a scrappy junco or a bossy nuthatch.

Later, in a more thickly settled corner of New England, this childhood pleasure was renewed by setting a birds' table every winter for thirty-six consecutive years. Between times I made several brief winter camps in the Canadian wilds, where a bountiful table was set outside my cabin window, and where at every midday halt on the trail the impromptu spread was half of my lunch crumbled on a slab of bark beside a cheerful fire. During all these winter seasons, when I know not how many thousand individuals of the feathered species were directly under my eye, I have never seen Teedeeuk begin a quarrel with any other bird, but I have several times seen one or another of them chivvy him away from the table.

It is doubtless true that a pair of mated jays will drive other birds away from the tree or the copse they have chosen as a nesting site; so also will robins or bluebirds, not because they are quarrelsome, but in obedience to an elemental sense of property rights which all birds and animals instinctively display.

As for nest robbing, only twice in a lifetime have I seen a blue jay eat eggs. On one occasion a jay with the secretive air of a born thief speared three eggs from a catbird's nest and one from a robin's nest before the mother birds discovered and chased him away. Because this personal observation seemed to back what most bird books said, in an earlier work I called Teedeeuk an inveterate nest robber, or words to that effect—an accusation which I now withdraw and vainly regret.

An honored acquaintance of mine, who has been a lifelong observer of birds, tells me that he once, just once, saw a blue jay throw fledgling sparrows out of a nest, apparently in sheer mischief, since he flew off without eating them. On the other side of the balance, I have in a single season kept tabs on twenty-odd nests near my home, including a jay's nest within fifty yards of where two pair of robins and a pair of mourning doves nested; and with the exception of a crow, caught and shot in the act, there was no nest robbing from the time eggs were laid until the young took to wing.

From several such recent observations it seems to me prob-able, though as yet far from proved, that as an old black bear will occasionally turn game killer, or as a house dog will occa-sionally turn egg stealer, so may an occasional jay "go bad" and by his evil doing bring discredit and a prejudice on all his kind. The following is a case in point, which serves only to sug-gest what an extraordinary thing an individual jay may do; but whether it should be regarded as an example of ready wit or of total depravity, no one can rightly tell. There are times when facts speak for themselves only to ask a question.

Far out in the lower half of Moosehead Lake is Gull Island, a densely wooded, lonely place, known only to the gulls that use it every season for a nesting site. I was hidden there one heavenly June morning, when the lake was too calm for fly-fishing, in the hope of learning by what strange sense or affin-ity a mother gull distinguishes her ill-visaged fledgling in a group of ten or forty others, all alike in size, shape, color, and reptilian ugliness.

The many nests, few with any semblance of a lining, were mere hollows in the gravel or holes among the rocks bordering the only cove where the sun shone all day long. One nest might hold an egg or two, with just the sun for brooding; from another a pinfeathered youngster would wobble on unsteady legs to mingle with his kind, thus early displaying the gull urge to gre-gariousness. Silence was the unbroken law, this breeding ground being the only place where gulls were not loudly scream-ing or softly *kuk-kuking* their emotions. Every now and then a mother bird would wheel in from the lake, drop lightly to earth, and go straight to a certain fledgling as if she not only knew him but remembered which one of her brood had last been fed.

The young, however, had so little discernment that a dozen

or more would hurry with open mouths to every returning bird. Gently the mother bird avoided or brushed them aside, until one open mouth rang a bell of affinity in her brain. Into it she hastily pumped a portion of half-digested food; then she was away to find a dead fish or a bed of fresh-water clams or a nest of sandpiper eggs. Two short minutes or a long quarter hour might pass before another gull wheeled in, to solve at a glance the same baffling problem of selection.

During one of these blank intervals, when nothing stirred but the fledglings, I caught my breath at sight of a blue jay in the middle of the nesting ground, the last place one would look for him or any other small intruder. Where had he come from so unexpectedly? And why did he stand there motionless, his head cocked to the opening where a returning gull would first be seen? Plainly he was on forbidden ground, and well aware of it; his lowered crest was enough to tell that he was spying or bent on mischief. Something else about him, perhaps his wary attitude, spoke of danger, as well it might. If he were caught here by a mother gull a twist of her terrible beak would take his head off in a twinkling, and everything but his feathers would go to feed her young.

I first thought that he was nest robbing, and this raised the question of how he would handle eggs that in his eye must have looked as if a behemoth had laid them. But though many were in sight he paid them no attention. Straight to a hollow containing two newly hatched birds he went, and as he walked alertly around them he stopped on either side to prod them with his bill. At his approach they opened their mouths wide; at his prod they snuggled down to earth, obeying the primal impulse of every helpless creature to be quiet at the appearance of an enemy.

After suspiciously eying the unresponsive things a moment, Teedeeuk hurried to a group of larger fledglings, which he kept prodding, prodding until one opened its mouth to pump up what had recently been pumped down. Young herons will thus get "seasick" when disturbed, and Teedeeuk evidently knew what he wanted and how to get it. Hastily he gobbled a morsel of the disgorged food for himself; then with a larger portion in his bill he flew to a spruce tree, where later I found his nest. Being at the moment too much interested in his comedy to spoil it by showing myself, I failed to see whether he was dutifully feeding his young or gallantly refreshing his brooding mate.

A pair of jays, like a pair of grackles, will occasionally nest near an osprey and largely feed their young on crumbs that fall from the rich bird's table. One summer, on Sugarloaf Lake in the Quebec wilderness, I watched a nest of Ismaques, the fish hawk, with unusual interest on finding that a pair of jays had nested in a crevice of the huge structure. Not only were they peaceable tenants but, whenever both ospreys were away fishing, one or another of the jays always acted the watchman. Every time I approached the nest, a cry brought the ospreys winging back at top speed.

Because gulls have no such happy family understanding with other birds, I was idly wondering by what happy chance Teedeeuk had learned how to make a fledgling gull unswallow its breakfast, and how a fledgling would feel about having the sins of parents thus visited on an innocent stomach—when suddenly there he was again on the forbidden ground. He was roughly prodding another group of fledglings, evidently expecting more food of the same kind, when he vanished like a wink. Hardly was he gone before a gull wheeled in from the lake to feed her young with no apparent suspicion that something was wrong, or sadly amiss, as one hungry fledgling might have told her.

To me the most significant feature of Teedeeuk's exit was not its haste, but its direction. Was it by accident or design, I wondered, that on finding himself in danger of being caught and followed he flew not to his high nest, as before, but held close to earth until he was hidden by the underbrush on another side of the nesting ground.

Teedeeuk's prime trait, I should say, is the curiosity which impels him to investigate everything that goes on in his neighborhood, and as far beyond as he can see or hear. All birds are instinctively curious, else the young would never learn anything by experience; but with Teedeeuk curiosity is the breath of life. You may prove this by whistling or yodeling in the woods. Almost invariably, unless some other bird happens to be at hand, the first to appear on the scene is a blue jay, his crest betraying his emotion as he seeks the cause of the disturbance. Tell him by a slight motion of your head, just enough to get his attention, and instantly his manner changes. A moment ago he was a feathered Paul Pry; now everything about him suggests the town constable with his accusative question, "What's going on here?"

Even in nesting time, the one season of the year when Teedeeuk is as silent or secretive as a crow, and for the same good reason of concealment, his curiosity is a light sleeper, very easily awakened; or so it was told me by the first pair of mated jays that ever I watched. Their nest was in a stand of young oaks where, only for the fun of it, I often teased them by crowing like a banty rooster. Something in that cocky call was as magnetic to their spirit as food to a hungry gizzard; for, without fail, Teedeeuk would come immediately to find out who made it. One source of endless pleasure on my part was that, on finding me, he never seemed to suspect anyone of fooling him but would go peeking and harking about the woods in search of that invisible bantam. Another item of interest was that his mate appeared to be quite as keen for news as he was but must remain on the nest—uneasily, judging by her crest— while he went blithely off to find it.

The same lively curiosity is evident whenever Teedeeuk flies in haste to answer a distress call, but seldom or never, so far as I have observed, does he gang up with other birds to chase a hawk out of the neighborhood or a blacksnake into the nearest rock pile. It is manifest in a more exciting way when crows are baiting an owl, but here again, although I have often seen Teedeeuk among those present, he did not risk his own fine feathers by taking part in the massed bedevilment. He will swoop at a prowling cat, apparently for the fun of seeing her jump. Once I saw him join his mate in bravely fighting off a crow that had taken one of the nestlings, but on other such adventurous occasions he seemed well content to play the role of spectator at a safe distance.

Two fields distant from my boyhood home lived a kindly neighbor, Henry Daggett, who every season raised a few hundred Brahma chickens. Some of his large flock gathered nightly in the chicken coop, but so many more had a propensity for roosting like their forebears that on a moonlit night every apple tree in his back yard-orchard looked like an enormous chrysanthemum plant bearing a multitude of white blossoms. Having no hunting instinct, Henry depended on me for help whenever a hawk or fox troubled his flock, and one early-autumn morning he called me over to say that something, he knew not what, was nightly taking his chickens.

I could guess what that "something" was, having heard a great horned owl boom his hunting cry in the dusk, and before nightfall a jump trap was set for him in accord with the owl habit of using any bare stub for a listening post. A length of two-by-four scantling was placed upright by nailing its butt to the trunk of a fallen apple tree. On top was a platform, just wide enough to hold the trap; below the trap a dead chicken with outspread wings offered a tempting bait.

A clamor of crows roused me before sunup next morning, such a mighty uproar that I ran to it half dressed. Either the owl's weight or the pull of its broad wings had brought the scantling to the ground, where he now stood with his back against the roots of the fallen tree, one foot in the trap, feathers bristled out enormously, yellow eyes glaring in impotent rage. Whirling madly over him like a storm cloud, full fifty crows were yelling their heads off in a frenzy of excitement. On the trunk of the fallen tree two hen hawks were silently awaiting their chance to strike or to escape; but whether they had come to deal with the owl or had been driven to bay by the crows was their own secret. Their big mistake had been to come down to earth, where every attempt to rise in flight was smothered in a tempest of black wings, striking beaks, and wild war cries.

A flash of blue caught my eye, and there was Teedeeuk, hiding in a tree that held no crows. Another flash of color, and another, as jays changed position to see better, until five or six were located behind the black rabble. Their voices were mute, their crests eloquent as they peered from behind a limb at the vociferous comedy. Not one came from his hide-out until I jumped the wall, when a sharp *dee-uk* rose above the deafening clamor. As at a signal for which they had been waiting, the hen hawks sped away, with the crows yelling after them, and behind the crows went all the blue jays for another act, I suppose, of the same free show.

And the trapped owl? He was big even for his kind, standing over two feet tall. About him was an air of age, of dark wisdom, of inbred savagery which made him the wildest bird I have ever known, the most fiercely resentful of every effort to tame him. For a month or more he was kept in a cage roomy enough to let him exercise a bit, with a many-branched root for a perch and a shrub or two for the ground cover. At every approach he would withdraw to his darkest corner, his eyes closed as if he could not bear the sight of me; but he watched through a slit, snapping his beak or hissing fiercely to take my attention until my hand reached for him, when he would strike with curved talons that were nearly two inches long, strong as steel, and sharp as fishhooks.

Although his appetite was beyond belief, never would he eat by daylight or even notice what was offered him. Into his cage went dead rats, cats, rabbits, fish from Whiting Pond, blacksnakes from an old cellar where these reptiles gathered to hibernate, late-season woodchucks that had fattened in our vegetable garden, chickens that had died of injury or disease— everything one could find or catch or beg from the neighbors, which for the first time made me aware of what a pair of horned owls must do to game birds and fur-bearing animals when they raise two or three nestlings to their own size.

One thing I wanted to know was how a horned owl breaks up his game, whether with beak or claws; but even when his food was given a semblance of life by someone dragging it in front of him at the end of a string, my captive paid no attention except to watch through slitted lids. Next morning no food remained, not a feather or a bone or a bit of fur. If he reserved any portion of a hen or a fattened woodchuck for another meal, no one ever found where or how he hid it.

Often in the late evening there came from his cage a low muttering of owl voices, but never the hunting cry of an old bird or the guttural hoo-hoo-hooing of the young. On stealing out I would glimpse only a shadowy motion that faded away into the darkness. Night after night this crooning dialogue was heard, until one morning when the cage was empty. A hole had been torn in a corner under the roof, with nothing about it to tell whether a way of escape had been opened by Kookooskoos himself or by the mate that came nightly to visit him.

To return to Teedeeuk, another characteristic, a natural supplement of the first, is his bent for telling the news like a town crier. At the winter feeding table, for example, when other feathered guests may be off guard while satisfying their sharp hunger, Teedeeuk is commonly the first to detect a distant hawk and cry the alarm. The other birds flit away into hiding—all but Teedeeuk, and to observe him now is to note a significant thing. If the hawk sails on into the blue, Teedeeuk whistles his mellowest *kloo-loo-loo*, as if to say that the danger is past; whenever the hawk circles wide around the yard, Teedeeuk follows, giving tongue on the trail. Somehow, by changing his tone or accent, he tells what he wants the other birds to know or at least what they seem to understand. Otherwise why should they pay no attention when two or three jays are crying aloud in the field, but take instantly to wing when the same *dee-uk, dee-uk* voices a different message?

This news crying, as I venture to call it, is most evident in late summer, a glad time when many birds are flocking and practicing wing drills for the autumn migration. Teedeeuk's own occasional changes of place, as when he drifts to escape extreme cold or to find more abundant food, are very quiet affairs, and perhaps for that reason the late-summer flock jubilation is to him all the more attractive. Whatever the cause, birds of any kind seldom gather in conspicuous number without a blue jay to keep tabs on their assembly.

One September, on a hilltop far from the nearest farmhouse, an immense flock of starlings were wheeling, veering, rising, and falling as a single bird in one of their amazing wing drills (why they should practice it so often, since they do not migrate, is another bird puzzle without an answer, unless it be sheer delight in massed motion). I was drawing near the thrilling spectacle, stealing from bush to bush for concealment, when a blue jay shot over my head with a sharp cry. Although the starlings were talking among themselves in that queer creaking or gurgling, they heard his alarm above their own noisy gabble and veered wide away to another part of the hill. And then from trees or bushes, here, there, yonder, several jays that had evidently been watching the play came out of hiding to follow the starling players.

In the depth of winter, likewise, when Teedeeuk is often the only bird to give color to the gray woods or a voice to the silent fields, you may witness the same curiosity followed by the same news crying. On a morning after a light fall of snow, you go out with fox hunters to a runway, one of the paths that every fox takes in crossing from valley to hill. The mellow bugle cry of the hounds fades into silence. The woods and fields are all still as you wait expectantly, hour after breathless hour, until faint in the distance sounds a trail song to make your nerves tingle.

The fox has turned, he is coming back, he is still far away; or so you think, hearing only the hounds, until yonder on the wooded hill a blue jay cries his tallyho. Again he sounds it, this time to the left; and now by his news crying you can trace every move of the fox as he draws steadily nearer. You expect every moment to see him on the runway, when at a sharp jay call over his head he turns before you get even a glimpse of him. And why did he turn away, leaving you with that all-gone feeling in the pit of your stomach?

It is supposed that, even as crows cry vengeance on a fox or bobcat, so their family relative the blue jay is impelled by fear or hate when he finds the same enemy afoot; which may be true, but I wonder. The only thing of which one may feel reasonably sure is that no prowler can come or go or rest in a blue jay's range without his knowledge. Wolves usually hunt by night and, after eating their fill, roam far away in obedience to some inner wisdom that warns them not to harry the same ground two nights in succession. Before daybreak, while jays are still asleep, they have selected a bed wherein to rest during the daylight hours; yet seldom have I jumped a wolf from his day bed without finding on the scene a blue jay that seemed to know all about it.

One winter night in Ontario, when the snow was four feet deep and the thermometer far below zero, a jubilation of timber wolves awakened me in my snug cabin. Before sunrise I found where a pack of wolves had killed and partly eaten a buck. During the next six hours I was keenly intent on a trail which led in a northwesterly direction, with many turnings aside to follow easy runways, yet always returning to the original course. Afternoon shadows were beginning to lengthen when the trail abruptly turned to a steep hardwood ridge, liberally sprinkled with clumps of dwarf laurel. Here was a perfect day bed, with laurel for concealment, a ridge top for shelter against a bone-chilling wind, and a wide outlook for any wolf that lifted a head above the low cover (these canny brutes do lift their heads at frequent intervals while resting).

I was climbing the ridge from leeward, with immense caution because timber wolves are perhaps the hardest of our native animals to stalk, when the flash of a blue jay's wing stopped me in my tracks. For a moment or two he flitted around me, silent at first, then he whistled a *kloo-loo-loo* in his town-constable way, as if asking my business. Getting no response, not even a wink, he flew ahead to cry *dee-uk, tee-dee-uk* over a thick laurel clump hardly fifty yards distant. So near after hours of trailing, and yet so far in a moment! On coming to the promising place, sadly knowing what to expect, I found eight empty day beds reeking of wolf scent and eight scattered trails pointing by long jumps into the distance.

One such experience indicates no more than that an odd thing may happen by chance, but hunters have repeatedly told me of similar disappointments when following a buck on a good tracking snow. Deer signs are just getting fresh, getting warm, when a blue jay appears from nowhere to whistle softly before flying on. The next thing heard from him is an alarm cry, followed by the flurry of a jumping buck. And the moral is, if I read it correctly, that Teedeeuk sometimes tells the news to good effect and that other birds or animals know when he tells them of an enemy at hand.

The western blue jay is more silent than the newsmonger of our eastern woods, which may be the result of living in a solitude so vast that a rooster seldom crows because, as I fancied, there is no other rooster near enough to hear and dispute the proclaimed opinion. The western jay is also more brightly colored, the blue of his back and wings having a luster like the glint of sunshine on still water. But that is all on the surface, and from a small acquaintance I should say that he and Tee-deeuk are twin brothers under their skins.

The place of our first meeting was on the south rim of the Grand Canyon, a lonely and stupendous scene, far removed from every beaten tourist path. Out from the canyon rim, without even a handrail for protection, juts a thin spear point of rock. From its tip one may look out on breath-taking grandeur, or straight down into a depth so remote that the bottom is lost in violet mist. Twice from that spear point I have looked down on what no man ever expects to see—the back of a soaring eagle.

One afternoon, while holding watch over a place that seemed to belong to me alone, a quick-moving shadow told of life on the wing, and I looked up to see a blue jay fly along the canyon rim before he turned into the pinewoods behind me. Placing two fingers against my lips, I pulled a breath between them to imitate the squeaky cry one hears when birds are having a tiff or calling for help. That call has been given in many places, at home or abroad, and everywhere it tells the same story, although it might be hard to put the story in words. I think it is only the projection of an emotional excitement to which birds instinctively respond, as to a crying of their young. Hardly had the call broken the enormous silence when a blue jay flashed out of the pines to answer it, not by his voice, for he said never a word during the interview, but by his bright questioning eyes and by his bodily attitude, which changed with his emotions as a weather vane turns to shifting winds. From branch to branch he flitted, stopping only long enough to peer and hark a moment before going on to ask and listen from another perch.

Getting no answer from the pines, he sailed down to the dizzy verge of the spear point, where he stood alertly at ease, peering many times up and around but never once down, as if he knew that the exciting call had spelled life, and that no life was possible beyond the canyon rim. It seemed that he must see me, sitting there within twenty feet; but in his eye I was only another rock, even when he flew over my head on his way back to where he had a mate and a nest. After a quiet interval of five or ten minutes another call brought him out to repeat the same fruitless investigation, and now as he held still for a moment he gave me a sign whereby to know him if we should meet again. One of the secondary quills of a wing was sadly awry, a result either of the long-gone molting season or of a heedless flight in thick cover.

While waiting expectantly for some other atom of life to companion me in the solitude, a thunderstorm rolled up, one of the violent Arizona downpours that in a half minute drench you to the skin. A low pine offered partial shelter from the rain, and with the sun I came out to resume my seat near the base of the spear point, hoping again to see what had once held me speechless—the full circle of a rainbow in the canyon depths.

The rainbow had formed, when a blue jay appeared on the scene—the same bird with his telltale wing. Almost in the middle of the spear point was a hollow, not much wider than my hat and perhaps two or three inches deep, which the rain had filled to the brim. Straight to it came my blue jay, as if he knew what he would find. Never have I seen a bird more plainly

happy, although he said never a word. All jays are fond of bathing, and this lone pilgrim was making the most of an opportunity which comes but seldom in that semi-arid region. In and
out he jumped, flitting his wings to splash water all over him,
making a thousand flashing jewels as the spray was pierced by
brilliant sunshine. He was drying himself at last, trying to do
something about that obstinate wing feather, when without
warning he flashed away as if frightened, taking the same line
of flight he had twice followed more leisurely.

I was wondering what had startled him, knowing that it was
no motion of mine, when back he came with another jay, his
mate presumably, who had all the while been brooding her
eggs. Like a gallant cavalier he stood aside while she enjoyed
her tub, splashing merrily, sending up more jewels and rain-
bows into the sunlight. Not until she came out for a preening
did he jump in for a second bath; another moment and both
were in the tub at once, flitting water with their wings as if
they could never have enough of its delicious coolness. Then
they stood silent awhile on the verge of the canyon, the glory
of creation round about them, before flying off together to their
nest in the pines.

Although birds lack our human gift of language, they have
another and perhaps surer way of sharing small thoughts that
have no outlet in emotional cries. It is, I think, by mutual sympathy, which alone gives perfect understanding without need
of our always imperfect and often misleading speech.

Young Wings Must Fly

ONE attraction of my fishing cabin is that relics of the hermit trapper who built it, years ago, still hang on its smoke-darkened walls. Weathered by sun and storm the cabin stands between the river and the evergreen forest in a natural opening where, for a reason that nature keeps secret, no trees grow but only an earth covering of native grass is brightened by the bloom of wildflowers. On the porch, content with the day's fishing, I restfully await the supper call, knowing that it will be late because two other sportsmen will stay out with their guide another hour or two in the hope of raising still another salmon. Meanwhile, having the camp all to myself, there is nothing to do but much to enjoy at a time and place so quiet, so blissfully serene that it brings to mind the fabled land where it is always afternoon.

Over there across the river is another wilderness pilgrim, much smaller than I but more fortunate, a pilgrim who does not have to wait for his supper but is blithely getting it for himself on the wing. By his motion I recognize him as a flycatcher of some kind; no other bird flies like that, as no other hovers like a hawk or teeters like a sandpiper. A proper ornithologist in my place would go over to name the bird in sesquipedalian verbiage or to collect his skin as a rare specimen, as if the identification of species were the only important matter. One might know everything of that external kind, yet understand nothing of bird life.

What interests me in my small neighbor is that every afternoon at this hour he flits up from where his nest is probably hidden to perch on the same stubby branch of a pine, whose dark crown towers above the surrounding forest. The air has its eddies and currents, just as the river or the sea. Insects are drawn to them as naturally as trout to a spring hole or salmon to a resting pool, and this bird neighbor of mine knows where to expect good hunting much better than I know when or where to find good fishing. Against the lowering sun his airy swoops after flying insects are as dark lines swiftly etched on gold; when he returns to his perch his form is as sharply outlined as a cameo cutting. At this distance I listen in vain for the crunch of his beak on a juicy morsel; but through my field glass his attitude, at once restful and alert, tells me that all is well with his world.

Leaving the flycatcher to his supper, I steal to the porch edge on hearing a slow, rhythmic *tunk-a, tunk-a, tunk-a,* prolonged into a sleepy kind of roundelay which seems to deepen rather than break the restful stillness. I hope to learn, at last, how a chipmunk makes that queer sound, so unlike a squirrel voice; but this is not my lucky day. At sight of me Chikooweesep, as the Malecites call him, whisks into his hidden doorway with a derisive whistle, as if to say, "Catch me doing it if you can!"

Down among some rocks that are well covered with earth, Chikooweesep has a den where he stores his food below the frost line, and where he eats or sleeps in comfort while winter storms roar overhead. His original entrance, made by tunneling from a distance, was carefully closed after he had made up his mind. Not until a chipmunk has settled in a den does he run a short tunnel up to the surface, throwing the loosened earth back among the rock crevices—which may explain why you find no sign of digging around his doorway. He carries whatever I give him to his storeroom, but although he occasionally sits on my knee to take food from my hand, never does he tell me how or why he makes the hollow tunking sound I have heard from others of his kind. The sound comes seldom in the morning, often in the afternoon, and always at a siesta kind of hour when the sun is warm and the winds are stilled.

A sudden whir of wings accompanied by a jingling of bird voices, unmelodious as a tambourine, calls my attention from the vanished chipmunk to the river, where a score or more of crow blackbirds (which the books call purple grackles) are perched on the bank above my overturned canoe. On the coast they are known as boat-tailed grackles because their long tails, slender near the body, broad at the tip, are supposed to serve as a rudder in flight; but after repeatedly watching them in a wind I am convinced that the overlong "boat tail" is a hindrance rather than a help. In colonial days they were aptly called maize thieves because of their habit of swooping down in a destructive horde, tens of thousands in a single flock, to pull up the sprouting corn in spring or to play havoc with the harvest in late summer.

A family group of blackbirds now appears on the handrail that tops the bank in front of my cabin. They are plainly a mother bird with her fledglings, all in a dingy summer dress. Finding the coast clear, not noticing the man who sits motionless on the shadowy porch, they drop lightly to the ground and approach my doorstep with their dignified crowlike walk. As they peer about for crumbs, which others of their greedy kind have long since eaten, I recognize one bird that was in my hand early this morning. His perilous adventure, for such it must have seemed to him, occurred as an unexpected part of his coming-out party—a vociferous affair of throaty gurgling, metallic kluk-kluking, and scandalized tsup-tsuping, which is staged whenever a new brood leaves the nest and the fussy mother calls in the neighbors to congratulate or give unheeded advice.

The nest in this particular comedy was in a fir tree behind my cabin. Three of the brood had been persuaded or cajoled to try their wings in flight, but the fourth obstinately refused to budge. In a peevish protest he seemed to be saying that the nest was the only place he knew or cared for, the gabby neighbors were a nuisance, and he wanted his accustomed breakfast. I could not see how they got him out at last, but in the midst of a gurgling uproar he slanted heavily to the ground, where he lay gasping, wings outspread, beak wide open, as if ready to give up his little ghost.

Obeying some imp of mischief who suggested that the dying fledgling should be comforted, I wrapped him in a bandana and climbed the fir tree. My ears were assailed by a tempest of neighborly opinion; not a voice was silent or flattering. Hiding behind the fir trunk, where the fledgling could not see me, I placed him tenderly in his familiar bed. And no sooner did he perceive where he was than with a loud squawk of protest he hurled himself into the air, as if the nest were the last place on earth where he wanted to be.

That same fledgling, wholly forgetful of his morning experience, is now on my doorstep. Once again I note the most striking feature of every grackle: his eyes, brilliantly colored, fiercely glaring, set in a sooty background that seems to intensify the startling effect. In their expression, savage as the glare of a goshawk, is something that is not of earth and has no hint of heaven. Mephistopheles would have had eyes like that when he came at midnight to claim his due from Faustus. But why did nature give it to this diminutive and harmless crow?

From a distance, through the medley of grackle gurgling, which to me voices a meaningless emotional excitement, comes a single note, low and sweet, which snaps me to attention like a bugle call. It is the voice of a mother partridge, or ruffed grouse, talking to her chicks and making sense in everything she says. Her brood was raised within a stone's throw of my cabin, which is in perfect accord with the partridge habit of selecting the edge of a clearing for a breeding site. This is done not only because of the abundant insect food but more, perhaps, because the clearing offers a greater advantage from the bird's viewpoint: a warm sun bath after a cold night, a scratchy dust bath when skins are itched by growing pinfeathers, and especially the wider outlook that all forest-born creatures seek at intervals as if they enjoyed it.

For three seasons past, to my knowledge, and for twenty more seasons as the guides tell, a partridge has raised her brood in this vicinity. Since their range is small—a half mile or less in any direction before it intrudes upon the range of another brood—the bird now talking may be a lineal descendant of partridges that were at home here before the white man came and before the Indian. The broods hatch out early or late, depending upon the arrival of spring, and are larger or smaller in number according to dry or wet weather, among other factors, when young birds chip the shell. During a rainstorm the mother shelters them under her body and wings; but they must seek food twice daily, and if they get wet while covered only with down many of them are not hardy enough to survive the chill. A few weeks later they stand in an erect posture during a storm, and the rain slides from their oil-covered feathers as from a roof, leaving their skins dry and warm.

One afternoon I met this local brood on the trail, and I counted a full dozen young birds, an uncommonly large number, before they glided like gray shadows into the underbrush. It was near sunset, so I followed at a discreet distance to learn where they roosted, and I almost bumped one chick with my hat before seeing him, so well was he hidden by drooping leaves. In the early-summer season and until the brood scatters in autumn, they gather nightly to sleep in a loose group, never crowded together but each on his favorite perch, seldom more than two in the same low tree. And these two, I think, are the same two that one sees staying close together when the brood spreads out to feed. As in other family groups, partridges seem to have their individual likes and companionships.

Meanwhile the old drummer partridge, who fathered this brood and then seemed to forget it, roams more widely by himself. At nightfall he seeks the edge of a clearing or an old road and rests on the ground close beside a root or stump where his dark quiet makes him an inconspicuous part of the sleeping earth. When winter comes, old and young alike commonly seek a night shelter in the evergreens; after a heavy storm they plunge into the snow and sleep as under a soft white blanket.

Now the voice of one bird mystifies me by telling her chicks something I have never heard before. She has many calls, varying from the low *kwit* of surprise to a loud squeal of anger, but there is a hint of trouble in the voice that sounds faintly above the ridiculous grackle medley close at hand. It is not the mother bird's contented prut-prutting which she uses in thick cover and which the young repeat like echoes with the apparent object of holding the brood together. It is not the sharp warning at which they crouch motionless, invisible, when a shadow of wings passes overhead. It is not the liquid bubbling, like air escaping from a decanted bottle, which precedes the sudden take-off in flight. Nor is it the dovelike *kroo-kroo* which summons the hungry brood to an anthill, to an overnight growth of mushrooms, or to a checkerberry patch with its spicy green leaves and its crimson drops. In southern New England this soothing *kroo-kroo* has a jubilant undertone at times when the chicks are pestered by wood ticks and the mother finds a luxuriant growth of skunk cabbage. Eagerly they eat the pulpy hearts that smell like mingled skunk and garlic. The odor spreads through their little bodies with the apparent effect of sickening the ticks, making them lose their grip and fall to the ground.

But the present call is different from all others, and I must find out about it if possible; for a foot-loose naturalist any new sight or sound is an invitation. Knowing that any sudden motion will spoil the play, I stalk the distant brood as carefully as if the next step might jump a bear. The mother bird stands with upstretched neck on the riverbank with half her brood around her; the others move restlessly under a fir where the trail emerges from deep shadow into the sunny opening. In the wondrous clarity of this late-afternoon light, the soft colors of the birds, their alert action, even their bright eyes and changing expressions are clearly revealed. Some discord or unwillingness, a rare thing in a partridge brood, seems to be at work among them. With full crops the young birds move naturally toward the roosting place, only to be recalled again and again. Uneasily they shift hither and yon, moved by impulses that call them two ways at once.

Slowly, by coaxing or warning or whatever it is that a mother partridge puts into her voice, she gathers them into a loose group on the riverbank, where they have no cover of any kind. Without another word or sound, not even a whir of stiff pinions, she glides smoothly across the river. Faintly from the distance comes an insistent *oowit, oowit,* bidding the young to follow. They hesitate, fearful of the wide expanse, as it seems to me, until one chick crouches, waits a breathless moment, lifts his tiny wings, and speeds like a bolt to the other side. By twos and threes the others take wing and vanish into the alders on the farther bank.

These partridge chicks are now about the size of robins, if you can imagine a robin with a pointed little stump, like a meadow lark's, where his fine tail should be. Up on the nearest hardwood ridge, chicks of equal size have been flying for a fortnight past, but although I have several times met this brood on the trail, never before have they used their wings. Being well fed, they did not cross the river for more food, nor were they frightened into flight by me. And when in the deepening dusk I stole to the roost, they were all resting in their accustomed place. The mother had made them cross forty yards of swift water, only to bring them back within the hour. But why? To see only the obvious fact of natural life may be to miss all that is worth seeing.

Unlike most other birds, partridges depend almost wholly on their legs for locomotion. Habitually they use their short wings on three occasions only: to flit into a tree before nightfall, to escape quickly when an enemy is too near to be avoided by running or hiding, and very rarely to seek a new range when driven from the old by hunger or disease or persecution by dogs and gunners. Hunters have a legend that ruffed grouse act crazily at times, and men even speak of a "crazy moon." But the legend rests, I think, either on the wildness of grouse, as of all other game, during a few autumn days when leaves are falling to a high wind, or else on the cock-grouse habit of seeking mates at a distance when they fail to come to his drumming log. At such times he drums by night as well as by day, and on moonlit nights especially. His ordinary flight, made when alarmed, is only from one part of his range to another, seldom more than a quarter mile at most. But here by my cabin an undisturbed hen grouse had led her chicks on a flight which must have seemed to them, as it did to me, quite needless.

The next afternoon at the same hour I was knee-deep in a salmon pool, about three miles upstream, when above the ripple of flowing water rose a sound even sweeter in my ear: the low call of a hen partridge to her brood, and the answering, "Here I am, here I am," a routine which is apparently intended to keep the chicks from straying too widely in thick cover. The bank behind me was grown to wild grass, and beyond this grassy fringe were dense alder thickets. No life could be seen, but a change in the tone of eager voices told that the partridges were coming out of deep-woods shadow into the sunlight, alertly, as always they move, and twistingly because of the many obstacles. Presently waves ran through the grass, little waves that talked as they ran, all heading toward a gravel bar at the lower end of the salmon pool.

Partridge talk is easily imitated, and at my coaxing invitation the rearmost wave turned in my direction. Out of the cover glided a young partridge, only to dodge back at sight of a stranger who made the mistake of turning to see him better. The grass was everywhere quiet until, at my repeated invitation, four chicks emerged to stand alert on the bank, their necks stretched to take the measure of a strange animal that was now harmless in their eyes because it stood motionless as a rock. A low word from the mother recalled them, and once more the grass waves ran all in the same direction, until the whole brood came out on the gravel bar. There without a moment's hesitation the mother flew across the river, making no whir of wings as she took the air. Unwillingly, as it seemed to me, the chicks followed her flight and vanished in the alders on the other side.

Here was the same puzzle, a well-fed brood crossing open water at an hour when other broods were more naturally moving toward the roosting place, picking up an odd morsel of dessert on their way. Less than an hour later, I was again fishing the pool when from the other side a hen partridge flew over, followed by her chicks. That it was the same family appeared more than probable by three considerations: the number of young birds was the same; they were of the same size and outward appearance; and it is very rare to find two broods on the same range at this season. And then, while my glance swept over river and valley and distant hills, an answer to the puzzle seemed to come from the smiling landscape itself.

Since early spring the weather had been very dry, and at a time of drought the only likely place to look for a partridge is in the vicinity of living water. Many had nested near the river, so many that nearly every salmon pool I fished, which was over twenty in a stretch of about nine miles, had a partridge brood in the neighborhood. Throughout that distance the banks were in most places thickly grown to alders, with here or there a knoll of spruce or hardwood, and this alder ground reached back from a few rods to a half mile before giving way to open growth. It was ideal nesting cover, offering not only food for the young but almost perfect protection from hawks and owls, which will not swoop into a thicket but wait and watch to catch their game in an opening.

Now a young partridge must quickly learn to use its wings, which is manifestly impossible where brush grows so thickly that even old birds cannot fly through the tangle but must rise above it for a straightaway flight. And to *rise* on its small wings is the last thing a young bird learns. Woodcock nested abundantly in the same alder cover, but even after the young were nearly full-grown it was difficult to make them take to wing. At my approach they would merely scurry into hiding. The mother bird, after waiting until she was almost stepped on, would rise above the alders, her broad wings flicking the many twigs, and drop back to earth a few yards beyond, where she would call the scattered brood together.

One afternoon, when coming down river with a Miramichi guide, we had the experience of a lifetime in seeing a woodcock brood cross in front of our canoe, and to our amazement they were swimming as easily as a family of ducks. Although the

young were larger than sparrows, which was certainly large
enough for flight in other breeding localities, they made no
attempt to use their wings when we followed them into the
grass, where we caught one and dropped him back in the river,
hoping to learn how he navigated so well. The mother woodcock circled overhead, occasionally sending one low call to her
hidden chicks and, as it seemed to me, a different call to the
captive in our hands. Hardly was the little fellow in the river
before he scurried to the bank and vanished, so quickly that
we could not clearly see how he did it. He seemed to be running
on the water, his motionless wings lifted and spread like tiny
planes.

Returning to the young partridges, my conclusion was that
the mother led them to the river because it was the only opening where they might safely try their wings. Other partridges
that nested back on the hardwood ridges, always near a brook,
found plenty of natural openings among the big trees. When
a brood was surprised on a logging road the mother was first
to take wing, heading for the nearest cover; following her went
the chicks, flying close to the ground at first, and gradually
learning how to rise in a high flight with the characteristic
whir of their kind. Down in the alder thickets, meanwhile,
where no bird could fly close to the ground without danger of
bruised or broken wings, every mother partridge seemed to be
leading her chicks to the river for their first flight. This was
either a bit of intelligence, or else, possibly, a remembrance of
how the mother bird had learned to fly in a forbidding environment.

The only objection to such a conclusion, on my part, is that
a wide stretch of flowing water would be a dangerous place for

a trial flight, the risk of drowning being much greater than that of bruised or broken wings. In any partridge family some chicks are bound to be larger and more vigorous or more gifted than others; and what must happen to a weakling that failed to make the whole distance from bank to bank? Several times that summer I stopped fishing to watch a partridge brood cross the river, and I always had the same doubt that it was done with an intelligent purpose and always I felt the same disturbing question of a weakling's fate.

The answer came on a day when, hearing partridge talk in the alders after a salmon had taken my fly, I pulled a lot of loose line from the reel in order to give the hooked fish my blessing to do as he pleased for a while. Once again, to my delight, little waves came toward me through the grass, with a bird voice under every wave. On the gravel beach were the alert forms of a mother partridge with her brood of ten chicks. Perhaps because of a later hatching they were decidedly smaller than the chicks near my cabin, so small that it may have been their first flight when they followed the mother bird across the river.

I was turning to my salmon when a troubled *kwit-kwit* sounded in the grass, and out ran still another chick, only to dodge back into cover at sight of me. He was plainly the smallest of the brood, probably the runt that so often appears in a large family. Either he had gone astray in the alders or had become tangled in the grass, and was now left alone in a big world for the first time. Twice my imitation of partridge talk lured him out, but he had seen me move and was afraid. On his next appearance he darted to the water's edge, where he stopped irresolute. From the other side came a low insistent call, faintly heard above the melody of rushing water. One could only imagine the impulse that swelled the chick's tiny body when at last he crouched and hurled himself into the air. The flight proved too much for such weak wings; he was still six or eight yards from the other shore when down he plumped into the salmon pool.

"It's all up with you now, poor little chick," I said mournfully, thinking that no land bird could swim in such fast water. The next moment I was swinging my hat in a silent cheer on seeing him spurn the current with kicking feet and flapping wings as lustily as a young sheldrake. Something like a brown streak twisted up into the alders, and he was gone to rejoin his family. And then it came to me with comforting conviction that a mother partridge seems to know what her chicks can or cannot safely do.

A last reassuring glimpse of that same brood was given me a week or two later. The water had by this time fallen to low summer level, and from the river below the salmon pool emerged a sandbar island. Wavelets ran merrily around it, and bubbles gathered into white foam patches tipped with brown. Fishing suspended for the midday rest, I was watching through my field glass a brood of woodcock resting in the middle of the little island. It was evidently their molting season, when these birds disappear for a time; they were now motionless except when one or another humped his back or turned toward the sun.

Grass waves ran through the cover behind me, and out came my brood of partridges, eleven of them, following the mother or running eagerly ahead. They were silent now, not a *kwit* or a *kroo* chimed with sound of the river. The water was shallow where they emerged from the grass, and they waded daintily from the bar to the upper end of the island and stood there in a close group, soaking up the sunshine with the molting wood-cock.

There was a ripple of waves in the river below, and out from a bogan where she had nested, a black duck led her brood to the lower end of the same little island, where they preened feathers, stretched wings, and twisted necks as if to get all the kinks out of them. They alone talked in a low gabble, which in the distance had an undertone of chuckling.

Woodcock and partridge and black duck warmed themselves peaceably together, sunshine full upon them, the river singing its song, the woods all still, no enemy to trouble or disturb their peace. And I had another living picture to store away in my fisherman's creel of happy memories.

Snowy Visitors

ONE stormy winter afternoon I was watching for black ducks by a lonely salt creek that doubled across the marshes from Maddaket Harbor. I had built my blind among some bushes in the shadow of a low ridge near the freshest water. In front of me a solitary decoy, having been confined all day, was splashing about in joyous freedom, quacking loudly at the loneliness of the place and at being separated from her mate. Beside me, crouched in the blind, my old dog Don was trying his best to shiver himself warm without disturbing the bushes too much.

It grew dark and bitterly cold. No birds were flying, and I had stood up a moment to warm my half-frozen toes, when a shadow seemed to pass over my head. The next moment there was a splash, followed by loud quacks of alarm from the decoy. All I could make out, in the obscurity under the ridge, was a flutter of wings that rose heavily from the water, taking my duck with them. Only the anchor string prevented the marauder from getting away with his booty. Not wishing to shoot, for the decoy was a valuable one, I shouted and sent out the dog. The decoy dropped with a splash, and in the darkness the thief got away—just vanished, like a shadow, without a sound.

The poor duck died in my hands a moment later, the marks of cruel claws telling me plainly that the thief had been an owl. I supposed that it was only a great horned owl, and so I laid plans to get him.

Next night I was at the same spot with some wooden decoys, over which the skins of wild ducks had been carefully stretched. An hour after dark he came again, attracted, no doubt, by my continued quacking. I had another swift glimpse of what seemed only a shadow; it poised and shot downward, striking the decoys with a great splash and clatter before I could find it with my gun sight. He had not discovered his mistake when I had him. The next moment Don came ashore, proud as a peacock, bringing a great snowy owl with him—a rare prize, worth ten times the trouble we had taken to get it.

Owls are generally very lean and muscular; so much so, in severe winters when food is scarce, that they are unable to fly straight when the wind blows; and a twenty-knot breeze catches their broad wings and tosses them about helplessly. This one, however, was fat as a plover. When I stuffed him, I found that he had just eaten a big rat and a meadow lark, hair, bones, feathers, and all. It would be interesting to know what he intended to do with the duck. Perhaps, like the crow, he has snug hiding places here and there, where he keeps things against a time of need.

Every severe winter a few of these beautiful owls find their way to the lonely places of the New England coast, driven southward by lack of food in the frozen North. In Massachusetts they prefer the southern shores of Cape Cod, and especially the island of Nantucket, where, besides the food cast up by the tides, there are larks and blackbirds and robins which linger all winter. At home, in the Far North, the owls feed largely upon hares and grouse; here nothing comes amiss, from a stray cat, roving too far from the house, to stray mussels on the beach that have escaped the sharp eyes of crows and sea gulls.

Some of this owl's hunting ways are most curious. One winter day, prowling along the beach, I approached the spot where, a day or two before, I had been shooting golden-eyed ducks over decoys. The blind had been made by digging a hole in the sand; in the bottom was an armful of dry seaweed to keep my toes warm. Just behind the stand was the stump of a ship's mainmast, the relic of an old storm and shipwreck, cast up by the tide.

A commotion of some kind was going on in the blind as I drew near. Sand and seaweed were hurled up at intervals, to be swept aside by the wind. I dropped out of sight into the dead beach grass to watch and listen. Soon a white head and neck bristled up from behind the old mast, every feather standing ferociously straight out. The head was perfectly silent a moment, listening; then it twisted completely around, to look in every direction. A second later it had disappeared and the seaweed was flying again.

There was evidently a prize in the old blind. But what was he doing there? Until then I had supposed that the owl always takes his game from the wing. Farther along the beach was a sand bluff overlooking the proceedings. I gained it, after a careful stalk, crept to the edge, and looked over. Down in the blind a big snowy owl was digging away, with first one foot, then the other, like a hungry hen, tearing out sand and seaweed with his great claws and sending it up in showers behind him over the old mast. Every few moments he would stop, bristle up all his feathers until he looked comically big and fierce, take a look out over the log and along the beach, then fall to digging furiously again.

I suppose that the object of this bristling up before each observation was to strike terror into the heart of any enemy that might try to surprise him at his unusual work. It is an owl trick. Wounded birds always use it when approached.

The object of the digging was soon apparent. A beach rat had jumped down into the blind to get some fragments of my lunch, and, being unable to climb up the sheer sand walls, had started to tunnel up to the surface. The owl heard him at work and started a stern chase. He won, too, for right in the midst of a fury of seaweed he shot up with the rat in his claws. Had it not been for the storm and his underground digging, he surely would have detected me long before I could get near enough to see what he was doing, for his eyes and ears are wonderfully keen.

In his southern visits, or perhaps on the ice fields of the Arctic Ocean, the snowy owl has discovered a more novel way of procuring his food than digging for it. He has learned to fish. Once on the north shore of Nantucket I saw him get his dinner in this way.

The bay was full of floating ice, and thousands of coots were swimming about the shoals. While watching them through my field glass, I noticed a snowy owl standing still and straight on the edge of a big ice cake. It looked as if he were trying to drift down close to the flock of coots before they saw him.

That was interesting, so I sat down on a rock to watch. Whenever I took my eyes from him a moment, it was difficult to find him again, so perfectly did his plumage blend with the white ice.

But he was not after the coots. Suddenly I saw him lean forward and plunge a foot into the water. Then, when he hopped back from the edge and appeared to be eating something, it dawned upon me that he was fishing—and fishing like a true sportsman, out on the ice alone, with only his own skill to depend upon. In a few minutes he struck again, and this time he rose with a fine fish, which he carried to the shore to devour at leisure.

For a long time that fish was to me the most puzzling thing in the whole incident, for at that season no large fish are to be found, except in deep water offshore. Some weeks later I learned that, just previous to the incident, several fishermen's dories with full loads trying to land through a heavy surf had been upset on the east side of the island. The dead fish had been carried around by the tides, and the owl had been deceived into showing his method of fishing. In his northern home, when the ice breaks up and the salmon are running, he goes fishing from an ice cake as a regular occupation.

The owl lit upon a knoll not two hundred yards from where

I sat motionless, and he gave me a good opportunity of watching him at his meal. He treated the fish exactly as he would have treated a rat or duck: stood on it with one foot, gripped the long claws of the other through it, and tore it to pieces savagely, as if it were a bit of paper. The beak was not used, except to receive the pieces, which were conveyed up to it by his foot, as a parrot eats. He devoured everything, even the bones, in great hungry mouthfuls. Then he hopped to the top of the knoll, sat up straight, puffed out his feathers to look big, and went to sleep. But with the first slight movement I made to creep nearer, he heard me and flew to a higher point.

The stomach of an owl is peculiar, since there is no intermediate crop, as in other birds. Every part of his prey small enough (and the mouth and throat of an owl are large out of all proportion) is greedily swallowed. Long after the flesh is digested, feathers, fur, and bones remain in the stomach, softened by acids, until everything is absorbed that can afford nourishment, even to the quill shafts and the ends and marrow of bones. The dry remains are then rolled into pellets by the stomach and disgorged.

This, by the way, suggests the best method of finding an owl's haunts. Search, not overhead, but on the ground under large trees, until a pile of these curious remnants of savage feasting reveals the nest or roosting place above.

It seems remarkable that my fisherman-owl did not make a try at the coots that were so plentiful about him. Rarely, I think, does he attempt to strike a bird of any kind in the daytime. His long training in the North, where the days are several months long, has adapted his eyes to seeing perfectly, both in sunshine and in darkness; and with us he spends the greater part of each day hunting along the beaches. The birds at such times are never molested. He seems to know that he is not good at dodging, that they are all quicker than he and are not to be caught napping. And the birds, even the little birds, have no fear of him in the sunshine; although they shiver themselves to sleep when they think of him at night.

I have seen snowbirds twittering contentedly near him. Once I saw him fly out to sea in the midst of a score of gulls, which paid no attention to him. At another time I saw him fly over a large flock of wild ducks that were preening themselves in the grass. He kept straight on; and the ducks merely stopped their toilet for an instant and turned up one eye so as to see him better. Had it been dusk, the whole flock would have shot up into the air at the first startled quack.

His favorite times for hunting are just after dusk or just before daylight, when birds are restless on the roost. No bird is safe from him then. The fierce eyes search through every tree and bush and bunch of grass. The keen ears detect the faintest chirp or rustle or scratching of tiny claws on the roost. Nothing that can be called a sound escapes them. The broad, soft wings tell no tale of his presence, and his swoop is swift and sure. He utters no sound. Like a good Nimrod, he hunts silently.

The flight of an owl, noiseless as the sweep of a cloud shadow, is the most remarkable thing about him. The wings are wonderfully adapted to the silent movement that is essential to surprising birds at dusk. The feathers are long and soft. The laminae extending from the wing quills, instead of ending in the sharp featheredge of other birds, are all drawn out to fine hair points, through which the air can make no sound as it rushes in the swift wingbeats. The *whish* of a duck's wings can be heard two or three hundred yards on a still night. The wings of an eagle rustle like silk in the wind as he mounts upward. A sparrow's wings flutter or whir as he changes his flight. Everyone knows the startled rush of a quail or grouse. But no ear ever heard the passing of a great owl, spreading his five-foot wings in rapid flight.

He knows well, however, when to vary his program. Once I saw him hovering at dusk over some wild land covered with bushes and dead grass, a favorite winter haunt of meadow larks. His manner showed that he knew his game was near. He kept hovering over a certain spot, swinging off noiselessly to right or left, only to return again. Suddenly he struck his wings over his head with a loud flap and swooped instantly. It was a clever trick. The bird beneath had been waked by the sound; with the first movement the owl had him.

All owls have the habit of sitting still upon some high point, which harmonizes with the general color of their feathers, and swooping upon any sound or movement that indicates game. The long-eared or eagle owl invariably selects a dark-colored stub, on top of which he appears as a part of the tree itself, and is seldom noticed; the snowy owl, whose general color is soft gray, will search out a birch or lightning-blasted stump and, sitting still and straight, hide himself in plain sight so that it takes a good eye to find him.

The swooping habit leads them into queer mistakes sometimes. Two or three times, when sitting still in the woods watching for birds, my head has been mistaken for a rat or a squirrel by owls which swooped and brushed me with their wings, and one left the marks of his claws before discovering his mistake.

Sometimes the crows find one of these snowy visitors on the beach and make a great fuss and racket, as they always do when an owl is in sight. At such times he takes his stand under a bank or in the lee of a rock, where the crows cannot trouble him from behind, and sits watching them fiercely. Woe be to the one that ventures too near! A plunge, a grip of his claw, a weak *caw*, and it's all over. That seems to double the crows' frenzy—and that is the one moment when you can approach the owl rapidly from behind. But you must drop flat when the crows perceive you, for the owl is sure to look for the cause of their sudden alarm. If he sees nothing suspicious, he will return to his shelter to eat his crow or just to rest his sensitive ears after all the pother.

And then a curious thing happens. The crows, which a moment ago were clamoring angrily about their enemy, watch with a kind of intense interest as you creep toward him. Halfway to the rock behind which he is hiding, they guess your purpose, and a low rapid chatter begins among them. One would think that they would exult in seeing him surprised and killed, but that is not crow nature. They would gladly worry the owl to death, if they could, but they will not stand by and see him slain by a common enemy. The chatter ceases suddenly. Two or three swift fliers leave the flock, circle around you, and speed over the rock, uttering short notes of alarm. With the first sharp note, which all birds seem to understand, the owl springs into the air and is off up the beach. The crows rush after him with crazy clamor, and speedily drive him to cover again—— But spare yourself more trouble. It is useless to try stalking any game while the crows are watching.

In Quest of Waptonk, the Wild

A vast and lonely barren, covered deep with soft-colored mosses and surrounded by gloomy spruce woods, lay basking in the early-morning sunshine. The first sea wind rolled up the mists that had covered it all night long, and under this vanishing coverlet the plain seemed to stir and breathe deep and stretch itself drowsily, like a gray wolf just awake. No sign of life moved on the tranquil face of the earth; no sound entered the restful stillness save a low surge drifting in over distant woods from where the waves broke on the unnamed shoals. And here was the end of my long quest to find the home of Waptonk, the wild goose.

Ever since childhood I had sought him. In the spring he had always called to me from the high heavens; and something in the ring of his bugle call and in the impulse of his wild heart found an answer in the heart of the boy who watched him. Unknown longings had bound me fast to Waptonk the Wild and made me resolve someday to follow him and find out what it was that called him northward when the big woods were budding and the spring impulse was in the heart of all living things.

Later Waptonk had called to me again, but then he pointed southward, and the flight was altogether different. The lines of the arrowhead wedge of the flock wavered and were often broken; they held closer to earth and were less certain in their magnificent onward rush; and the clear full-throated bugle calls gave place to a curious communicative chatter, in which almost every note rose at the end to a falsetto. Now and then a strong, clear note, deeper and more peremptory, would sound at the head of the wedge, and instantly the wings would cackle an answer and swing into better line; but the cry had lost much of its joy and utter freedom, as the flight had lost its power and swift certainty.

I did not know then, in the autumn, that these were mostly young birds which had never before followed the long trail and that at the head of every wedge was one of the old birds, pointing out the headlands by which they shaped their course. The flight was less certain because the goslings had not yet reached their full power and must rest by the way, and the cry was less stirring because spring no longer called them away to its throbbing love life and the quiet nesting places in the far Northland. In the fall they were driven away from the things they loved, and the security of the great, free wilderness must give place to constant watchfulness in a hostile land, where danger lurked and roared out upon them from every bay and feeding ground.

Then in those autumn days the boy felt the hunter stir within him, and the wild-goose call from the heavens came down to him as a kind of a challenge. When the weather was stormy and the flight was low, the boy would climb stealthily out of the rear window of the barn with the forbidden old musket close to his breast. He would head across the brown fields to the woods, on his way to the little Widow Dunkle's, who kept an old gray goose. Sometimes he begged, sometimes he bribed, and sometimes, when the flight was irresistible and the widow away from home, he simply appropriated what he wanted with all his heart. Then the boy would scoot and dodge away to the big pond in the woods, with the old musket at trail and the old gray goose gripped tight under his elbow, *konk-konking* her resentment, but sensible enough, as all geese are when you take them right.

Hidden in the grass and bushes of a lonely point, the boy scanned the heavens, and in front of him an old gray goose, with one foot anchored to a brick, swam about and tilted her tail to the skies as she splashed and probed the bottom for roots, gabbling to herself in her wonder and delight at her strange surroundings. When at last the wild geese came, how the centuries of domestic servitude fell away from the old gray-lag! Tugging at the stupid brick with outstretched neck and quivering wings, she recognized her people and sent up a wild cry to call them down to share her loneliness. And the boy, holding his breath and loving the old goose supremely for her help, lay still as a stone, his eyes following the flight of the wild birds to see if they would come down to his bidding.

But the wedge kept steadily on, straight and true to its course, although every head was bent to bugle down an answer to the captive. The boy's heart was touched in watching his old graylag. Beating her useless wings, struggling after her kindred as far as the anchor string would allow, she would call and call, and all the wildness of the lonely Northland was in her appealing summons. Long after the clangor had died away, she would sit listening with neck upstretched, hearing, and in her heart answering, the call. After that there was no more joyous gabbling from Graylag. She swam about silently, pecking angrily at the restraining string, raising her head to look and listen for her wild kindred until twilight fell sadly on the pond and she went home again mute and passive under the boy's arm.

One stormy day great luck came to the boy. A large gang of wild geese, flying lower than usual, with the sides of their wedge broken by the sleet, and irregular from weariness, passed near the pond on their southern migration. Their faint, confused honking roused all the wild longing in the heart of Old Graylag. And something in their call, which she seemed to understand, made her sure they would come this time, and that she would know at last what the longing in her old heart meant. As she raised herself on her poor wings and sent out her clamorous appeal, the wild leader stopped, and the long wedge seemed to tumble together in a dense mass of cackle and confusion. Then the leader whirled; above the clamor came the deep honk of authority; the lines formed swiftly, with marvelous precision, and straight up the pond to the boy's hiding place they came, a glorious big wedge of birds, honking in joy at so good a resting place and nearly taking the heart out of Old Graylag as she tugged at her anchor and beat the water with her wings.

Then, all by himself, the boy saw a bit of Waptonk's drill school which old goose hunters on the coast have looked for many years in vain. High overhead the birds came until they were over the middle of the pond, when the leader whirled sharply to the right. The right-hand side of the wedge whirled after him; the left wing halted and then turned in behind the leaders in a single long line. Every wing was now set stiffly; the clangor suddenly ceased and down they came, around and around in a beautiful spiral, as if they were sliding down an invisible winding staircase. The long, magnificent line swung in a complete curve above the leader and half around the circle again; all with set wings and outstretched necks, gliding, wheeling steadily downward in perfect order and perfect silence.

The grace, the precision, the impressive silence of the stately procession down the spiral staircase of the winds were marvelous, and the boy forgot the hunter in his intense wonder and admiration. One by one the great birds dropped their black-webbed feet for a brief moment, and then dropped with a quiet, restful splash into the water. An instant later they had swung together and a low, eager chatter began among them.

Old Graylag had been unimpressed by the wonderful descent, for other things were stirring in her lonely heart. All the time they were coming down, she kept up a hysterical cackle, with a wild beating of pinions and a frantic tugging at the anchor as she strove mightily to join her kindred. As they swung together with their necks up suspiciously (for no wild waterfowl likes any welcome or demonstration beyond the universal uplifting of wings) she ceased her wild struggle and called softly. Instantly the leader answered and the whole flock drew in steadily toward the shore.

Behind the rough screen of grass and bushes the boy's heart began to beat loudly as he clutched his long musket. The hunter was wide-awake again, and here were the geese, almost within gunshot, drawing steadily closer and calling as they came on, great splendid birds that never before were nearer than the heavens. In front of him the old gray goose jabbered back at the flock and swung rapidly in small circles about her anchor. Her excitement increased; the flock halted, wavered, veered aside; then the heart of the old goose went after them in a wild, breaking *honk!* There was a tug, a plunge, a flurry of wings; the anchor string snapped and away she went, half flying, half running over the water, and plunged in among the wild birds in a smother of spray. In an instant she was swallowed up in a dense circle of gray backs and slender black necks with white cheek patches, and the whole flock drew swiftly away into open water, cackling and jabbering softly, with the nasal *konk-a-konk* of Old Graylag sounding incessantly above the hushed chatter of her wild kindred.

Late that day, after waiting long, cold hours in the vain hope that they would come near my hiding place, I sadly pushed out in a leaky old tub of a boat to catch the Widow Dunkle's goose. The flock took alarm while I was still far away. It slanted heavily upwind to the treetops, where with much calling and answering the young birds fell into line, and the wedge bore away swiftly seaward. After them went heartbroken Old Graylag beating her heavy way over the water, calling and calling again to the flock that had now become only a confused tangle of wild voices over the treetops. She went straight to the shore and across a little wild meadow, still following the flock. When I caught her she was waddling bravely through the woods, stopping to call and listen; but she made no resistance when I tucked her under my elbow and carried her home and slipped her, unobserved in the darkness, into her accustomed place in the Widow Dunkle's duck coop.

That was the nearest I ever came, in boyhood days, to a close acquaintance with Waptonk the Wild. Later I grew acquainted with many of his winter ways; I watched him feeding on the shoals or standing for sleep on the lonely sand bars, and I thrilled to the rustling sweep of his broad wings as he swung in over my decoys. But always in the fall his voice aroused the hunter as no other sound ever did; and always in the spring his clanging jubilate aroused the longing in my heart to follow after him and find out what it was in the wild, lonely North that called him.

The trained geese which were often used as decoys—descendants of sundry wing-tipped or wounded birds that had been saved to breed in captivity—were very different from Old Graylag. When the honk of wild geese was heard and the long wedge wavered over the pond, these trained birds would be loosed to circle far out from shore and with a wild clamor call down their wilder kinsfolk. Then slowly, cautiously, as if they knew well the treacherous work they were doing, they would lead the wild birds in toward the blind within range of the hidden gunners, when they would scatter suddenly and rush aside to get out of the way; and the decoyed and wondering geese would be left open to the murderous fire of the concealed hunters. An evil work, it seemed to me, and I am glad to remember I took no part in it beyond that of watching with intense interest and wondering at the cunning patience with which an old pothunter had trained his wild confederates.

Watching these trained decoys, it was hard to realize that the birds had been the wildest and wariest of all the feathered folk. Then the startling paradox occurred to me that the very wildest of the creatures are the easiest to tame by man and the quickest to adopt his ways. The sparrows that live about our houses all their days have little fear of men, but at the first attempt to catch them they are suspicious for life, and to domesticate them would be an impossibility. So it is with the ruffed grouse—in his native wilderness a very tame bird that barely moves aside to let men pass, yet all attempts to domesticate him or to make him content with safe quarters and abundant fare have been, with a few rare exceptions, unaccountable failures. He lets you come near to watch him readily enough, but the moment you put him in your coop the very spirit of wildness takes possession of him and he dies in the attempt to regain his freedom.

On the other hand the wild goose, the most fearful of birds when he comes among us in his migrations, gives wide berth to everything that has the least semblance to man or man's invention, and never lets you get within rifleshot if his wary sentinels can detect your approach. But he will feed from your hand after he has been a few hours in a coop, and his descendants will take a permanent and contented place in your barnyard. In the spring, when the migratory fever stirs within him, he will answer the clarion call of his fellows in the sky and spread wide his wings to join them, but that passes speedily, and he turns back to your dooryard and seems content even with the clipped wing which keeps him there while his brothers and kinsfolk fade away in the cold blue distance. There have been cases in which a wounded goose, having been kept all winter, has flown away with a passing flock into the unknown North during the spring migration and returned the next fall to the same barnyard, bringing her brood with her.

The first great lesson I learned in the years of following the wild goose as a hunter was one of tremendous respect for his wariness and intelligence. To call a person a goose would be an exaggerated compliment or a bit of pure flattery, if one only understood what he was saying. Wherever Waptonk feeds in the open, he has sentinels—wise old birds that know their business—posted on the highest point of observation, and it is next to impossible to approach a flock without being detected. On the coast he still listens to the voice of his kind and comes to the trained decoys, and on the prairies a deep pit with wounded birds tied to stakes all about it and honking to their fellows will sometimes bring him near enough for a quick shot. But these unfair advantages are in themselves a confession of man's failure; even by his own wit and with the advantage of modern firearms he is no longer able to contend with the intelligence of a goose.

Elsewhere, especially in the great wheat fields of the Southwest, there is a humorous example of man's impotence and Waptonk's superiority. Here horsemen go shooting and shouting about to frighten away from the growing wheat the thronging thousands of wild geese that cannot be circumvented or destroyed. And the most ridiculous thing in the whole proceeding is that the goose cavalryman must fume and fret under the thought that the exasperating birds understand him perfectly. They feed and gabble away serenely, paying no more heed to him than to any other scarecrow, until just before he gallops up or foolishly tries to creep within range behind his horse, when the sentinel gives the alarm and the whole flock takes wing and settles down comfortably to feed in another part of the same wheat field.

This is the more remarkable in view of the fact that this marvelous shrewdness with which Waptonk evades the best inventions of men is far from being a matter of instinct; it is imparted to him on the spot by his wise old leaders. For untold

generations he has been born and bred in the waste places of
the North, where he sees no man and where his life is singularly
carefree and fearless. When, full-grown and strong of wing, he
starts southward for the first time, he knows absolutely nothing
of the world of men. Left to himself and his own instincts he
would speedily tumble into the first cunning pitfall, but, fortunately for the young goose, his parents always lead the flock
of which he is a part. From them and from the old leaders,
trained in the school of long experience, he speedily learns to
shift for himself and to make his own way in a world of wits.

All these and many more things the boy learned as he followed Waptonk with the hunters, but his chief question remained unanswered. From books and baymen alike he heard
the same story: how the honking wedge might be called down
to decoys and how the wary birds might be tolled or trapped
or outwitted and killed. But what Waptonk was as a living
creature, what thoughts were in his head and what feelings
in his heart when he was far from men in his own home where
he could be himself—that problem nobody answered. Something to be killed, rather than a living thing to be known and
understood, was what met the boy at every turn. And always
in the spring, when the wild call of the voyagers floated down
from the blue heavens and the boy's eyes followed eagerly the
rush sweeping northward to love and liberty, something new
and strange stirred in the boy's heart and made him long to
follow.

It was, therefore, only the fulfillment of many years of ex-
pectancy, when I crept out of the low spruces away up on the
northern peninsula of Newfoundland and found the end of my
long quest. A subdued chatter of wild voices had called to me

softly above the steady murmur of the river as I stole through
the woods in the early June morning. Following the sounds,
which faded away like a will-o'-the-wisp when I tried to find
them, I was led away from the river and out of the big woods
to an unknown barren; and there, close at hand in a little
flashet, was Waptonk the Wild, waiting quietly as if he had
always expected me.

Still and secret as my approach had been, Waptonk had been
watching me for some moments before I saw him. He was a
splendid big gander, with a soft gray body that almost lost its
outlines against the gray shore; his glossy black neck stood
straight up from the water, and a pure white cravat rose on
either side of his cheeks, like the immaculate "choker" of the
old-fashioned New England minister. All the wildness and wariness seemed to have fallen away from him. He looked at me
steadily, quietly, without fear; there was a certain sense of dignity in every strong, graceful line of his body, and an unmis-
takable sense of his responsibility in guarding that which was
hidden away somewhere on the farther shore. My first thought
was: Can this be the same bird that I have followed so long
in vain? There he sat, calm, self-contained, without a tremor
of fear or curiosity, and with no intention, as far as my eyes
could discover, either to approach or to fly away.

I carefully drew near and sat down on the shore, while Waptonk swung easily back and forth on a short beat in front of me.
As the minutes passed and I made no hostile sound or movement, he increased his swing until it covered an irregular half
circle whose center was a point on the farther shore; I knew
then where I should find his nest and gray mate. Presently
he began to talk, a curious low gabble. Out of the grass and
moss on the point a head and long dark neck rose to look at

me steadily; near it were low cheepings and whistlings, where the goslings had been hiding in silence until the danger passed by.

Having found his secret, I made my way around the pond. Waptonk stopped his patrol to watch me a moment, then followed closely, keeping just abreast of me as I made my slow way along the treacherous bogs. When I doubled the end of the little pond and drew near to where his nestlings were hidden, Waptonk turned to the shore and hurried ahead of me to his mate. He stood over her reassuringly, bending to intertwine his neck with hers and to rub his cheek softly over her wings with a gesture that could mean only a caress; his head bent lower still to touch for an instant the goslings that were hiding in the moss. Then he left them abruptly and rushed to where I was standing watching the amazing scene, and he drew up defiantly, squarely across my path.

A thrill of admiration ran over me as I looked down at him standing there so strong and confident, ready to defend his own. "You splendid fellow; you brave knight!" I kept saying to myself. But I wanted to test him farther, and especially I wanted to see all that was hidden in the gray moss, so I started forward again cautiously.

At the first step a lightning transformation swept over Waptonk. Big as he was, he ruffled all his feathers and half spread his great wings until he looked twice his own size and formidable enough to scare any prowler. Another step; his eyes flashed, and he lowered his head and black neck close to the ground as he rushed straight at me, hissing like forty snakes, and with a gasping, terrifying cackle in his throat, as if his rage were choking him.

It was a magnificent, swift change from quiet dignity to the

raging defiance of an enemy ten times his size. The fierce hissing
got into my nerves, in spite of myself, and made me wonder if
any wild animal—living constantly, as animals do, on the thin
edge of flight and panic—could stand up against the terrifying
sound for a moment. Like a man caught in a fault, I had absolutely no defense; Waptonk was on his own ground, and I
had no business whatever in meddling with his affairs. To
throw myself upon him and by brute force to overcome the
noble fellow defending his little ones was out of the question;
it was plainly as impossible as to rob a bird's nest or to beat
a child. If I tried escape, hopping over the bogs, with the old
gander nipping at my heels and spanking me with his broad
wings, it would be an inglorious defeat. That was too much,
even for the sake of encouraging Waptonk as he deserved; so
instead of running away I sank down quietly in the moss, waiting half humorously to take my medicine and fully expecting
to get it "good and plenty."

He stopped quite near me, his head down close to the ground,
his tongue bent up like a spring into the roof of his mouth,
hissing vigorously and watching me keenly out of his bright
eyes to see the effect of his demonstration. I realized instantly
why he bristled his feathers and raised his wings, while he carried his neck and head down close to the ground like a big
snake. The wings, his only weapons, were half raised for a
blow, but the hissing yet harmless head would surely hold the
attention of any attacking animal. Any wild creature brave
enough to attack would naturally avoid the snakelike hissing
and leap over it for the larger body, only to be met by a stinging
blow in the face from the powerful wings. If the delicate neck
were carried high, an animal would naturally leap for it, and
Waptonk's fight would be over almost before he could strike

a blow. As it is, Waptonk carries his most vulnerable point as close to the ground as possible, and by scaring an enemy with his snakelike hiss he gets a fair chance to use his weapons and so takes care of himself splendidly against all prowlers.

Waptonk was evidently amazed at my quiet. Having expected either fight or flight, he was thrown off balance and hardly knew how to meet the emergency. He kept his defensive attitude a moment or two until the hissing gradually died away. Suddenly he raised himself and threshed his great wings in my face. I could feel the strong wind of them on my cheek and measure the nervous muscular beat under his feathers as he tried their power. Then he put his head down to the ground and hissed again, daring me to come on.

Ten yards behind him sat his mate, her head raised out of the grass, watching us steadily without a sound. Then she uttered a low call with a curious accent of warning and reassurance. It was a communication to her champion, plainly enough, for he wavered slightly for the first time from his intense attitude. The next moment she slipped out of the grass into the pond, and after her came five goslings, alert little bundles of yellow-brown fuzz; they walked steadily across the shore with a funny effect of carrying their knees up close to their shoulders, and glided easily into the friendly waters. There was another low call from the gray mate; then Waptonk, though he had not turned his head nor taken his keen eyes for an instant from my face, turned swiftly aside and threw himself into the water. A push or two from his powerful webs, and he was floating safely far beyond my reach, still looking back at me alertly over his shoulder as he surged away.

The little family glided swiftly along the pond shore, the mother leading them and talking to them reassuringly. Between them and me hovered Waptonk, swinging back and forth on his watchful patrol, until they disappeared from sight; then he glided silently after them into a muddy lagoon where the treacherous bogs forbade any human foot to follow.

An hour later the little wild family stole shyly out of the haven where they had hidden and found me sitting quietly just where I had first appeared. If they were surprised or uneasy, they gave no sign of their feelings beyond a bright, inquisitive look; they swam slowly past me and climbed the bank where it was worn hard by their feet, and started across the barren on their day's foraging. For hours I followed them, keeping out of sight as much as possible, watching with keenest interest their feeding and discipline, and noting especially the crude beginnings of that wedge formation with which they would later make their first long flight southward ahead of the autumn gales.

Wherever they went, Waptonk, the big gander, was near them, hovering on the outskirts or watching over them keenly from every little hillock that commanded a wider view of the great barren. He ate little and apparently only incidentally. His whole business seemed to be to guard his little flock, while the mother led them about to feed or trained them to the perfect discipline that is the wonder of all those who have ever watched wild geese. When at midday the feeding was done and the goslings were sunning themselves on the bank of another flashet under the mother's eye, Waptonk took wing and bore away swiftly over the woods and marshes to the ocean; as if in his cramped life he wanted room and exercise, or perhaps just a glimpse of the wise sea, which he loved. Within the hour he was back again, standing guard over his own.

Later, as I returned day after day to watch the gray voyagers that had so long attracted me, I saw a rare bit of Waptonk's care and sagacity. One of the goslings, more headstrong than the others, had wandered away from the leader over a treacherous bit of bogland and found himself slogged in some soft mud that he attempted to cross too hurriedly and carelessly. He floundered desperately for a moment, called sharply, and then lay perfectly quiet with his wings extended on the mud to keep himself from sinking deeper. Instantly the mother bird called all the young close about her, raised her neck high to look at her helpless gosling, then turned her head and honked deeply to the gander. Waptonk had already seen the danger from his vantage point and rose heavily in the air. Circling once over the little fellow in the mud, as if to measure the situation, he turned and flapped over him, reaching down to seize a wing in his bill. With the youngster kicking vigorously and flapping his free wing to help himself, he half dragged and half carried his careless offspring over the mud and hiked him out upon the moss with a final unnecessary jerk that seemed to tell him roughly to take better care of himself another time. But he lowered his head to rub his cheek softly down the little fellow's neck and over his wings again and again before he walked quietly away to his post as if nothing whatever had happened.

Then came the final scene, which only increased my strong desire to understand what passes in the heads and hearts of the wood folk. The mother went to the careless one and brought him back to where the flock was waiting. Standing in the midst of her brood, she seemed to be talking to them, first in a low chatter, then in a strange silent communication in which not a muscle moved, but every neck was raised in the attitude of intense attention. A moment later the flock was moving across the barren, cheeping, whistling, feeding as before.

In the afternoon, as I watched by the home flashet, there was another scene altogether different; and here were many things that a man could not be expected to understand, although I saw and admired them often enough. As the sun sank and the pointed shadows of the spruces came creeping out across the barren, the little flock wandered back, as is the custom with wild geese, to spend the night by the nest where they were born, to sleep contentedly under their mother's wings while the old gander kept watch in the darkness. Waptonk is more of a land bird than any of the ducks. The forward set of his legs shows that nature intended him to walk as well as swim; and he will never sleep in the water if he can find a safe and quiet spot to rest on the shore.

At sight of the familiar place the little family that I had watched all day long suddenly stopped their hungry wandering and came running in a close group, heads up and whistling, tumbling down the slope and throwing themselves with glad splashes into the friendly water. They drank and washed themselves and played together in little races and scuffles; they stopped their play to stretch their necks down to the oozy bottom for roots that they had overlooked or for earth and pebbles to aid their digestion. As the shadows lengthened they glided to an open spot on the bank to preen and gabble softly; the big parent birds, their own preening done as they watched the play of their little ones, went from one to another, rubbing them tenderly with their white cheeks, chattering over each one in turn, and in many little indescribable ways showing their fondness—their gladness that the long good day was done and they were safe at home once more.

Here before my eyes was a little family that had come back in the sunset, after much wandering and some danger, to the one spot in the great wilderness that they knew well, where life began for the goslings, and where each familiar thing seemed to welcome them and make them feel at home. Over them stood the parents, strong and watchful against the world, but tenderly telling their little ones by the soft caress of their cheeks that they loved and understood them. The twilight stillness was filled by a low, contented gabble, unintelligible perhaps, yet telling plainly by its changing accents the goslings' many feelings from the day's bright excitement to the evening's sleepy content.

A great tide of light rolled suddenly over the plain from the west as the clouds lifted, and the young birds stopped their chatter to turn their heads and watch silently for a moment as the glory swept over them. The voices were different, more hushed and sleepy, yet with a slight note of wonder, when I heard them again. In the nearest thickets a choir of thrushes was ringing the Angelus; a solitary vesper sparrow, hidden in the gray moss, sang his hymn to the evening; a fox barked in the distance; the river hushed its roar as the night fell, and went singing down on its way to the sea. And to all these sounds, to every wave of light and passing shadow and restless wing of the eddying plovers, the young birds responded instantly with low cheeps and whistles, drawing nearer and nearer together to feel a last touch of their parents' white cheeks. I lay and watched them, for nature reveals not only herself, but some beautiful and forgotten part of man's own soul, when she finds him responsive in the wilderness.

Slowly the glory deepened and faded, and the crimson flush that had spread wide over the great barren went creeping back into the West. After it came the silence, hushing the goslings' chatter and the birds' hymn; only the river was left singing to itself through the listening woods. Over the vast plain the fleecy mists that I had seen rise at dawn settled softly again to cover the sleeping earth like a garment. I could no longer see the birds that I had followed all the long, sunny day; but where the little family stood a soft gray shadow blurred the open shore. From it came now and then a sleepy, inquisitive peep as some little one stirred uneasily; a deep, quiet voice answered to tell him that all was well and that he was not alone in the darkness.

That was my first real meeting with Waptonk, my first answer to the question which had always been in my heart. And I was satisfied, perfectly satisfied, as I turned away in the twilight across the wild barren to where my little tent by the salmon river was waiting.

A Wild Duck

TO most people a wild duck suggests a line across the autumn sky at sunset, or a dark triangle moving southward, high and swift, at Thanksgiving time. To a few, who know well the woods and fields about their homes, it may suggest a lonely little pond, with a dark bird far out of reach, rising swiftly, leaving ripples playing among the sedges. To those accustomed to looking closely it will suggest five or six more birds, downy little fellows, hidden safe among roots and grasses, and so still that one seldom suspects their presence. The duck, like most game birds, loves solitude. He keeps the details of his life very closely to himself, and we must be content with occasional glimpses.

This is especially true of the dusky duck, generally known among hunters by the name "black duck." Only as you follow him winter after winter, meeting with much more discouragement than success, do you pick up many details of his personal life; for wildness is born in him, and no experience with man is needed to develop it. On lonely lakes, in the midst of a Canadian forest, where he meets man for the first time, he is the same as when he nests at the head of some millpond within sight of a busy New England town. Other ducks may, in time, be tamed and used as decoys; not so he. Several times I have tried it with wing-tipped birds, but the result was always the same. They worked night and day to escape; they refused all food and even water until they broke through their pen or were dying of hunger, when I let them go.

One spring a farmer whom I know determined to try with young birds. He found a black duck's nest and hatched the eggs with some others, under a tame duck. Every time he approached the pen the little things skulked away and hid; they could not be induced to show themselves, although their tame companions were feeding and running about quite contented. After two weeks, when he thought them somewhat accustomed to their surroundings, he let the whole brood go down to the shore just below his house. The moment they were free the wild birds scurried away into the water grass, and no amount of anxious quacking on the part of the mother could bring them back into captivity. He never saw them again.

This habit, which the young birds have, of skulking away out of sight, is a measure of protection that they practice constantly. In the early spring a brood may be seen on almost any secluded pond or lake in New England, where the birds come to build their nests. Watching from some hidden spot on the shore, I have seen them diving and swimming about, hunting for food everywhere in the greatest freedom. The next moment they scatter and disappear. If you are near enough you may hear a low cluck from the old bird, who sits with her neck standing straight up out of the water, so still as to be easily mistaken for one of the old stumps among which they are feeding. She is looking about to see if the ducklings are all well hidden. After a moment there is another cluck, very much like the first, and the downy little fellows come bobbing out of the grass or from close beside the stumps where you looked a moment before and saw nothing. This is repeated at frequent intervals to accustom the young birds to hide instantly when danger approaches.

So watchful is the old bird, however, that trouble rarely threatens without her knowledge. At the first sign of the enemy, when the young are well hidden, she takes wing and leaves them, returning when danger is over to find them still crouching motionless in their hiding places. When surprised she acts like other game birds: flutters along with a great splashing, trailing one wing as if wounded, until she has led you away from the young or occupied your attention long enough for them to be safely hidden; then she takes wing and leaves you.

The habit of hiding becomes so fixed with the young birds that they trust to it long after the wings have grown and they are able to escape by flight. Sometimes, in the early autumn, I have run the bow of my canoe almost over a full-grown bird lying hidden in a clump of grass. A month later, in the same place, the canoe could hardly approach within a quarter of a mile without his taking alarm.

Once they have learned to trust their wings, they give up hiding for swift flight. But they never forget their early training and, when wounded, they hide with a cunning that is remarkable. Unless one has a good dog it is almost useless to look for a wounded duck, if there is any cover to be reached. Hiding under a bank, crawling into a muskrat hole, worming a way under a bunch of dead grass or pile of leaves, clinging to a root under water, swimming around and around a clump of bushes just out of sight of his pursuer, diving and coming up behind a tuft of grass—these are some of the ways by which I have known a black duck to try escape when I was looking for him.

With the first sharp frost that threatens to ice over the ponds in which they have passed the summer, the inland birds betake themselves to the seacoast, where there is more or less migration all winter. The great body of ducks moves slowly southward as the winter grows severe; but if food is plentiful they winter all along the coast. It is then that they may be studied to the best advantage.

During the daytime they are stowed away in quiet little ponds and hiding places, or they rest in large flocks on the shoals, out of reach of land and danger. When possible, they choose the former because it gives them an abundance of fresh water, which is a daily necessity, and because, unlike the coots which are often found in great numbers on the same shoals, they dislike tossing about on the waves for any length of time. But late in the autumn they desert the ponds and are seldom seen there again until spring, even though the ponds are open. They are very shy about being frozen in, and prefer to get their fresh water at the mouths of creeks and springs.

With all their caution—and they are very good weather prophets, knowing the times of tides and the approach of storms, as well as the days when fresh water freezes—they sometimes get caught. Once I found a flock of five frozen into the thick ice while sleeping, with their heads tucked under their wings. At another time I found a single bird floundering about with a big lump of ice and mud attached to his tail. He had found the insects plentiful in some soft mud at low tide, and stayed there too long with the thermometer at zero.

Night is their feeding time; on the seacoast they fly in to the feeding grounds just at dusk. Fog bewilders them and no bird except a plover likes to fly in the rain because it makes their feathers heavy, so on foggy or rainy afternoons they come in early or not at all. The favorite feeding ground is a salt marsh, with springs and creeks of brackish water. Seeds, roots, tender grasses, and snails and insects in the mud left by low tide are their usual winter food. When these grow scarce they betake themselves to the mussel beds with the coots; their flesh in consequence becomes strong and fishy.

When the first birds come in to the feeding grounds before dark, they do it with the greatest caution, examining not only the little pond or creek, but the whole neighborhood, before lighting. The birds that follow trust to the inspection of these first comers, and generally fly straight in. For this reason it is well for one who attempts to see them at this time to have live decoys and, if possible, to have his blind built several days in advance, in order that the birds which may have been feeding in the place shall see no unusual object when they come in.

By moonlight you may sit on the bank in plain sight of the decoys and watch the wild birds as long as you will. It is necessary only to sit still. But this is unsatisfactory; you can never see them well enough to know just what they are doing. Once I had thirty or forty close about me in this way. A sudden turn of my head, when a bat struck my cheek, sent them all off in a panic to the open ocean.

A curious thing about these birds, as they come in at night, is their power to make their wings noisy or almost silent at will. Sometimes the rustle is so slight that it is scarcely audible; at other times it is a strong *wish-wish* that can be heard two hundred yards away. I can only suggest that it is done as a kind of signal. In the daytime and on bright evenings one seldom hears it; on dark nights it is very frequent and is always answered by the quacking of birds already on the feeding grounds, probably to guide the incomers. How they do it is uncertain; probably in some such way as the nighthawk makes his curious booming sound—not by means of his open mouth, as is generally supposed, but by slightly turning the wing quills so that the air sets them vibrating. This can be tested by blowing on any stiff feather.

On stormy days the birds, instead of resting on the shoals, light near some lonely part of the beach and, after watching carefully for an hour or two, to be sure that no danger is near, swim ashore and collect in great bunches in some sheltered spot under a bank. It is indeed a tempting sight to see perhaps a hundred of these splendid birds gathered close together on the shore, the greater part with heads tucked under their wings, fast asleep. Scattered along the beach on either side are single birds evidently acting as sentinels. The crows and gulls are flying continually along the tide line after food; and invariably, as they pass over a flock of ducks, they rise in the air to look around over all the bank. You must be well hidden to escape those bright eyes. The ducks understand crow and gull talk perfectly, and trust largely to these friendly sentinels. The gulls scream and the crows caw all day long, and not a duck takes his head from under his wing; but the instant either crow or gull utters his danger note, every duck is in the air and headed straight offshore.

The constant watchfulness of black ducks is perhaps the most remarkable thing about them. When feeding at night in some lonely marsh, or hidden away by day deep in the heart of the swamps, they never for a moment seem to lay aside their alertness nor trust to their hiding places alone for protection. Even when lying fast asleep among the grasses with their heads hidden, there is a nervous vigilance in their very attitudes, which suggests a sense of danger. Generally one has to content himself with studying them through a glass, but once I had a very good opportunity of watching them close at hand, of out-witting them, as it were, at their own game of hide-and-seek. It was in a grassy little pond, shut in by high hills, on the open moors of Nantucket. The pond was in the middle of a plain, a hundred yards from the nearest hill. No tree or rock or bush offered any concealment to an enemy; the ducks could sleep there as sure of detecting the approach of danger as if on the open ocean.

One autumn day I passed the place and, looking cautiously over the top of a hill, saw a single black duck swim out of the water grass. After a few minutes of watching, he went into the grass again and I started to creep down the hill, keeping my eyes intently on the pond. I was halfway down when another duck appeared, and I dropped flat on the hillside in plain sight. Of course the duck noticed this. There was a commotion in the grass; heads came up here and there. The next moment, to my great astonishment, fully fifty black ducks were swim-ming about in the greatest uneasiness.

I lay very still and watched. Five minutes passed; then quite suddenly all motion ceased in the pond; every duck sat with neck standing straight up from the water, looking directly at me. They were so still that they could easily have been mistaken for stumps or peat bogs. After a few minutes of this kind of watching they seemed satisfied and glided back, a few at a time, into the grass.

When they all were gone I rolled down the hill into some tall grass at the edge of a little run. Then it was easier to advance without being discovered, for whenever a duck came out to look around—which happened almost every minute at first —I could drop into the grass and be out of sight.

In half an hour I had gained the edge of a low bank, well covered by coarse water grass. Just below me, within six feet, was a big drake with his head down, drawn so close to his body that I wondered what he had done with his neck. His eyes were closed; he was fast asleep. In front of him were eight or ten more ducks, close together, all with their heads under their wings. Scattered about in the grass everywhere were small groups, sleeping or pluming their glossy feathers.

These were the first black ducks that I had ever seen unaware that they were watched, and there was great satisfaction in thinking how completely they had been outwitted at their own game of sharp eyes. How they would have jumped, had they known what was lying there in the grass so close to their hiding place! At first, every time I saw an eye wink or a head come from under a wing, I felt myself shrinking close together in the thought that I was discovered; but that wore off after a time, when I found that the eye winked rather sleepily, and the necks were taken out just to stretch them, much as one would take a comfortable yawn.

Once I was caught squarely, but the grass and my being so near saved me. I had raised my head and lay with my chin in my hands, deeply interested in watching a young duck making a most elaborate toilet, when from the other side an old bird shot into the open water and saw me as I dropped out of sight. There was a low quack which brought every duck out of his hiding, wide awake on the instant. At first they all bunched together at the farther side, looking straight at the bank where I lay. Then they drew gradually nearer until they were again within the fringe of water grass. Some of them sat quite up on their tails by a vigorous use of their wings, and stretched their necks to look over the low bank. Just keeping still saved me. In five minutes they were quiet again.

Two or three hours I lay thus and watched them through the grass, spying very rudely, no doubt, into the seclusion of their home life. As the long shadow of the western hill stretched across the pond, the ducks awoke one by one from their nap and began to stir about in preparation for departure. Soon they were collected at the center of the open water, where they sat for a moment very still, heads up and ready. If there was any signal given I did not hear it. At the same moment each pair of wings struck the water with a sharp splash, and they shot straight up in that remarkable way of theirs, as if thrown by a strong spring. For just an instant they seemed to hang motionless in the air, high above the water, then they turned and disappeared swiftly over the eastern hill toward the marshes.

Kookooskoos, the Great Horned Owl

KOOKOOSKOOS is one of the names given by the Indians
to the great horned owl, the most destructive killer of birds,
small game, and fur-bearing animals to be found in our woods.
Countryfolk call him the hoot owl, forgetting that the barred
owl is a louder and more frequent hooter. Both are so silent by
nature that you may camp for a week or a month in the northern wilderness without hearing a word from them. Then one
evening for some unknown reason—possibly an atmospheric
change—they shatter the restful silence by a cacophony of
whooping, yelling, and idiotic laughter. At such a time I have

heard a horned owl bark gruffly like a dog, or a barred owl utter a prolonged howl like that of a timber wolf. Such outcries are probably for convivial occasions; at least, by imitating them you can bring the uncanny birds whooping around your campfire.

On other evenings the big owls utter only an occasional hunting cry, which is used apparently to frighten hidden game into betraying sound or motion. After sounding a call the owl bends forward in an attitude of listening, which may be seen in the twilight or, more rarely, on a cloudy day. But in the darkness it is by their hunting calls alone that you may know one unseen owl from another, as surely as it is possible to distinguish the whistle of a quail from the prolonged whistle of a meadow lark.

The hunting call of Kookooskoos is a deep, strongly cadenced *whoo, hoo-hoo-hooz, whooz, whooz*—the same six notes uttered in half as many seconds on the same pitch but with different pauses, different inflections, and a curious buzzing in some of its vowel sounds. The first booming note is rather startling to one who hears it for the first time; it sounds as if an unseen sentry were challenging from the darkness, "Who goes?" The next three, much shorter and so closely run together that often they sound like two with a catch of breath between, have to my ear a suspended inflection, as if asking, "Do you hear me?" The last two, each longer than the first, are even more challenging, more peremptory, demanding an instant answer.

It is vain to attempt to put such a call into our language or letters, but anyone who hears it will recognize the voice of Kookooskoos and be able to distinguish his hunting call from his many other outcries. The latter, expressions of individual moods or emotions, run up and down the scale from guttural to falsetto, with a sound of *hoo-hoo-hoo* to *waugh-waugh*, while the hunting call, being typical of a species, is always and everywhere the same, excepting only the occasion when a young owl tries it and fails.

After hearing the perfected call hundreds of times from southern New England to Labrador, I have tried.to analyze it first from the owl's viewpoint, and then to interpret it objectively; that is, by the impression it makes on a man who hears it as a measure of its probable effect on its intended victim.

One thing about the hunting call which mystifies me is that it has a hooded quality which makes it impossible to locate by ear alone, as if a ventriloquist were playing his tricks. Only when you see Kookooskoos as he sounds the call can you be sure where he is; and then, to your further bewilderment, he is much nearer than you thought. Does he deceive also the birds, hares, and squirrels, making them think he is so far away that they have ample time to escape, when in reality he is near enough to swoop at their first motion?

What may be the right answer is given by Kookooskoos himself whenever he changes his ordinary way of hunting—a stealthy way as we shall presently see—and sends out a penetrating call that warns all wild ears of danger. His perch is usually a tall stump overlooking an opening where small game is more abundant than in the deep woods. Like other owls and hawks, he does not willingly enter brushy cover but waits for the chance to catch his game where he will not bruise his broad wings by swooping. Before sounding the call he sits quiet for a time, so motionless that even to a keen eye his soft-colored body appears to be a part of his watchtower. The moment his challenge rolls over the woods he becomes alive and alert, indicating by his tense attitude that he is ready to strike at anything that stirs below.

Although he sees equally well by day or night, like his relative the snowy owl, Kookooskoos has the limitation of all natural creatures in associating life with emotion, and so he overlooks even a man who knows how to become a part of the environment by holding still. To my mind, his day vision is rather ordinary, not to be compared with that of a goshawk, and his huge wings make him so clumsy of action that seldom does he strike his game at the first swoop. Once in winter I saw him stoop five or six times at a dodging gray squirrel in a leafless tree, and then the squirrel escaped into a knothole. His hearing, by contrast, is perhaps the most acute to be found in the bird world, and the explanation is easily discovered. His ear openings are enormous, extending halfway around his big head; stretched across them like a gauzy curtain are delicate bristles to catch the faintest vibration of air and carry it to wide-branched filaments of the auditory nerve.

This marvelously sensitive ear might of itself be enough to tell why Kookooskoos tries at odd times to flush his game by a hunting call. Whether he does it intelligently or instinctively no one knows. But observation shows that if no response comes to his challenge he flies on silent wings to a stub overlooking another clearing and there repeats the call, more plainly or more faintly according to the direction of his flight. At the final scene, rarely witnessed by human eyes, all one's sympathy goes out to the innocent or foolish victim. Disturbed by the booming challenge a rabbit stirs a twig underfoot or a bird rustles a leaf, and on the instant Kookooskoos swoops, his terrible claws extended to strike.

Anyone who hears such a call with understanding is bound to try to harmonize such a complexity or apparent contradiction in the natural world with some fundamental simplicity of plan or unity of purpose. My own philosophy of the hunting call regards it as but another of the delicate balances between hunter and hunted which fills the natural world of birds, animals, and insects. On one side of the equipoise, nature has given the owl a night-seeing eye and an incredibly sensitive ear; on the other side nature has provided that hunted creatures are practically invisible to wild eyes and wholly inaudible to wild ears so long as they remain quiet. On one side the owl sounds a hunting call to startle any nearby bird or animal into a sound or motion that must betray its whereabouts; on the other, all harmless creatures are endowed with a compelling impulse to be still as a stone when first alarmed, thus protecting them from discovery. Such a fair balance between hunter and hunted appears to be as natural as life itself, forever poised for an up or down turn.

Less puzzling to me than the ventriloquism of the hunting call is the way Kookooskoos apparently times it to his purpose or, it may be, to the right atmospheric conditions. I have never heard the sound on a windy or a stormy night; never in the cacophony of hooting and gurgling of horned owls in social assembly. To appreciate what I venture to call the timing of Kookooskoos, let's examine first a few of his ordinary hunting habits.

Kookooskoos is a glutton; his feeding is so voracious and often so unclean that, to judge by a few examples I have known, no caged owl of his kind ever seems to get enough food to satisfy him. When hungry after long fasting he kills the first small living thing he meets—jay, crow, grouse, rabbit, mink, muskrat, snake, frog, domestic cat—and gobbles every scrap of it. In an hour or two, he disgorges feathers, fur, and cracked bones in the shape of dry pellets and is ready to eat again. If absolutely famished he may tackle even a porcupine; sometimes a horned owl, thin as a scarecrow, is found with a score of barbed quills stuck in his mouth and throat. In early spring, when skunks come out of their winter dens and all game is scarce in the big woods, almost every horned owl trapped or shot has a skunky odor to tell what he has hunted. At other seasons of plentiful game he may kill a dozen birds or squirrels in succession and eat only the heads and brains, leaving the rest to scavengers.

Except during a blizzard, when all wild creatures keep to their dens, Kookooskoos hunts practically every night of the year and all night long when greedy owlets must be fed. Naturally you would expect that his hunting call would be sounded constantly after dark, yet days may go by without its being heard. Occasionally but very rarely the call is heard on a dark day; which means, I think, that Kookooskoos knows where game is hidden and is trying to scare it into a betraying motion, as the snowy owl claps his wings over a white ptarmigan crouched invisible in the snow. During the summer and early fall he often keeps watch by day over a clearing where young partridges come at regular hours to feed or to dust themselves, and at such times he is as silent as the hawk that has an eye on the same toothsome game. Likewise, when Kookooskoos finds a brood of wild ducks he often watches from a hidden perch until they come within striking distance; and here again he is as stealthy as any other hunter, knowing that to alarm the game is to miss his chance.

The close of an August day found me on a stranded log below a salmon pool on the Tobique, waiting for a beaver family that for a week past had been coming regularly to dine on the bark of poplar boughs which I cut fresh for them every morning. It was just before sunset; the skies were aglow, and the river muted its cheery voice the better to hear a thrush sing evensong.

Into this heavenly quiet rushed a flock of half-grown sheldrakes, as noisy and restless as kingfishers. At one moment they glided smoothly upstream, breasting the stiff current as easily as water sprites; at the next they darted hither and yon as if witch-ridden, crinkling the river's face into foamy wakes, shattering the silence with a croaking of unmelodious voices. Leading the riotous procession was a mother bird, her brown head with its slender beak turning like a weather vane in shifty winds as vainly she tried to keep tabs on her uneasy brood. Following singly or in ever-changing clusters came twenty-eight young.

These unwelcome intruders turned my thoughts to the hundreds of beautiful young salmon they had eaten since morning —a day's total probably greater than the number of grown fish caught here by fly-fishermen during a whole season. Then, as the unnatural size of the family group became more apparent, I recalled an unrecorded sheldrake trait which for the time changed a fisherman's old hostility into a new sympathy tinged with admiration.

Several times I had witnessed a hawk swoop on a sheldrake brood. At sight or sound of stooping wings the mother flapped away with a loud splashing and croaking to hold the hawk's attention while the young dipped out of sight, if they were old enough, or sneaked into hiding if they had not yet learned to dive. The old birds are first to be killed, as a rule, being more conspicuous because of their self-sacrifice. Should the mother be caught at such a time, her young join another brood, where they are received and treated as equals, with the result that one often sees two or three or five broods with only one mother bird to lead them to good fishing pools by day or to safe lodging at nightfall.

Just as these oncoming sheldrakes were opposite me, giving no heed to what they thought a harmless bump on a log, a broad-winged shadow fell upon them, and away they scurried under a smother of upflung spray. The shadow was cast by Kookooskoos, who had all the while been watching the brood from a poplar over my head. At his second try, after clumsily missing the first, he picked up a young bird, killed it by a single grip, and carried it limp to the other shore. There on the gravel he tore his game to pieces and swallowed it in wolfish gulps, head, feet, wings, and all, leaving only a few loose feathers to tell the night wind of his silent hunting.

That many outcries of Kookooskoos can be accurately located by ear points to the possibility that the ventriloquism of his hunting call is a kind of vocal masque which he dons or puts aside at will. He can be very varied and uncanny in voicing owlish emotions.

On a summer journey my companion and I camped one evening near the Square Forks of the Saevogle in New Brunswick. Our tent was pitched by the river in a natural opening surrounded by noble evergreens. Around us the night fell, dark, cloudless, intensely still. A few stars winked mistily. In the air was that strange feel of hollowness which presages a storm and magnifies every tiny sound, as if the heavens were a shell.

We were sitting by our campfire, silent as old comrades are

at such an hour, when from out of the trees came a shriek—loud, prolonged, bloodcurdling—which for a moment froze us. Then we were on our feet, both staring at the same spot, in our eyes a question that neither could answer. Never in our wilderness wandering had we heard an outcry like that, nor anything to compare with it in stark ferocity.

Our first thought was of a panther or catamount, because we could think of no other beast capable of such a feline screech, and we were within the limit of his extreme northern range. And I remembered the catamount tales heard in boyhood—tales handed down in my native New England village, every one with a scream out of the darkness to make cold shivers run up one's back. My imagination pictured a catamount grown bold enough to stalk us; and one way of dealing with a stalking beast of any kind is to put fear into him by making him think he is the stalked rather than the stalker.

Loading our only weapon, a light shotgun which my scientific comrade used for collecting rare specimens, I strode out beyond the blinding campfire circle where the beast could see me coming; all I could hope to see of him was the shine of wild eyes flashing back the firelight. With an appearance of boldness that was sheer bluff I crossed the opening and entered the woods, now dark as a pit. The only thing that human eyes could see, by looking up, was a ragged patch of sky framed by the darker bulk of treetops. I stopped there, peering for an eye shine, when another shriek doused me with ice water. It apparently came from overhead; and I had my first inkling of what game other than a catamount might be afoot. Against the sky a shadowy something moved swiftly, blotting out the misty stars. Before it vanished I had swung the gun muzzle ahead of it and squeezed the trigger, not consciously aiming, but pointing by instinct.

The roar of gunpowder, deafening yet somehow comforting in that dark pocket, was followed by a swish, a thud, a gasping outcry. From another direction came a whispery sound, half heard, to which I paid no attention. Phil came running with our only lantern, and by its feeble light we found a horned owl flat on his back, fierce eyes glaring, wide-opened mouth hissing his defiance. Savagely he struck at a stick held down to him and bent his powerful legs to drive the talons deep. By his own dying grip we carried him back to our campfire.

The night was now still and our fir-bough bed inviting, but sleep was slow to come. Was it indeed Kookooskoos who challenged the first campfire he had ever seen, or some larger prowler that escaped unseen in the darkness?

A very different meeting, some twenty years later, brought a queer fellow feeling for Kookooskoos, making me momentarily forget the ruthless killer that every game protector shoots on sight if he can. It was nearly the end of winter when horned owls, who mate so early in the season, must brood the eggs at all hours lest they be buried by a snow squall or turned to marble by sub-zero cold. The place was Algonquin Park, Ontario, an immense preserve swarming with game, where I had come by invitation to suggest a remedy for timber wolves that were destroying far too many deer and fur-bearing animals.

At sunrise on a cold and brilliant morning I was following a wolf trail that led southward, at first, to where the pack had killed a buck and eaten their fill of venison, then westward as the brutes roamed far away to another hunting ground where they would rest until nightfall and where I hoped to surprise them in their day bed. For me that tireless wolf journey spelled tough travel because of a recent ten-inch fall of powdery flakes that covered three feet of settled snow; at every step a white wave broke over the snowshoe rims and had to be lifted for the next push ahead. After four or five hours of this, the trail entered a wide expanse of caribou bog, heading for some wolf rendezvous in the hills beyond. Having no more hope of running into this pack before nightfall, I turned and headed northeast on a short-cut across the huge bend of the back trail, hoping to strike the home lake at its head, near our cabin. And my first glimpse of the lake from the summit of a ridge told me that I had hit it below the outlet a mile or more from my objective.

With immense relief now, knowing the locality, I could "rest a pipe," as the voyagers say, while stretching the snowshoe cramp out of tired legs, and perhaps hear from some near or distant ridge an awakening clamor of wolf voices that would tell me where to look for a fresh trail next morning.

Twilight was beginning to creep up the hillsides, a brief and threatening pause, as if a measureless brush were drawing a chill shadow between the day with its invitation to come out-of-doors and the night with its warning to seek shelter. The big woods were seemingly deserted, lifeless. With the oncoming of twilight all the animals were at rest.

The surrounding forest was wholly quiet when a shadow moved swiftly amid the massed tree trunks, with another shadow close on its trail. Up and down, in and out, and round-about they whirled with perfect precision, meeting here, separating there, coming together again as if moved by a single impulse. Such a play of shadowy wings, accompanied by a hoo-hooing that ran up and down the gamut of owl expression, could mean but one thing: Kookooskoos was staging his love comedy, the first of its kind I had ever seen.

Horned owls mate for life, it is said, and the old birds were already nesting, as I knew. The pair before me, probably owlets of last season, were going through the ritual of a first courtship as if they somehow remembered every requirement of wing or voice or posture. From their first appearance the female, to judge by her larger size, had led the chase as if she expected to be caught. Down to earth she fluttered at last, followed closely by the male, only to find that soft snow and forest litter hindered their action. By a short flight they were out on the ice of the lake where footing was better, although it was still surprising that they could move freely or even stand comfortably on their hooked talons.

For a long moment both birds crouched motionless face to face, their feathers ruffled, wings spread, a few feet of gray ice between them. With a grotesque solemnity they began a forward-and-back measure like an old-time reel; forward by hop-hop until their beaks touched, return by hop-hop to crouch again with outspread wings. At every pause their heads bobbed in unison. In their fierce eyes was a strange glow; from one or another rose the low crooning of an owlish love song.

I was waiting for the final scene, hoping to learn whether big owls mate in the air, as eagles mate, when they moved shoreward under drooping balsam boughs. Only the male could be seen as he folded his wings, smoothed down his ruffled plumage, and stretched and stretched his neck high, like a wild duck on guard. Slowly at first he began to sway his stiffened body from side to side, then faster with a wider swing, like a pendulum turned upside down.

Every such ritual of bird courtship probably has some deep

biologic meaning, if one could search it out. This unnatural body swaying might bring the enraptured pair to the surrender point, I thought, knowing how easily birds are dazed by any motion that upsets their delicate sense of balance. Eager to see whether the female also was doing the topsy-turvy pendulum or only watching it in the other, I left my perch on the fallen tree—too soon. The ritual was not yet ended, and the chance of a lifetime was lost. At my first creeping motion a twig snapped, a small sound, but more alarming to wild ears than a gunshot. Both birds sprang aloft, their broad wings threshing heavily, silently, and they together vanished into the evergreen cover beyond the outlet.

Killooleet, Little Sweet-Voice

THE day was cold, the woods were wet, and the weather was trying patience and temper sorely. Fishing had been poor down in the big lake, and there were signs of civilization here and there, which we did not like; so Simmo and I had pushed up-river, thirty miles in the rain, to a smaller lake, where we had the wilderness all to ourselves.

The rain was still falling, the lake was white-capped, and the forest was all misty and wind-blown when we ran our canoes ashore by the old cedar that marked our camping ground. First we built a big fire to dry some boughs to sleep upon; then we put up our houses, Simmo a bark *commoosie*, and I a little tent. I was inside, getting dry clothes out of a rubber bag, when I heard a white-throated sparrow calling cheerily his Indian name, *O hear, sweet Killooleet-lillooleet-lillooleet!* The sound was so sunny, so good to hear in the steady drip of rain on the roof, that I went out to see the little fellow who had bid us welcome to the wilderness.

Simmo had heard it too. He was on his hands and knees, with just his dark face peering by the corner stake of his *com-moosie*, so as to see better the little singer on my tent. "Have better weather and better luck now. Killooleet sing on ridge-pole," he said confidently. Then we spread some cracker crumbs for our guest and turned in to sleep until better times.

That was the beginning of a long acquaintance. It was also the first of many social calls from a whole colony of white-throats that lived on the mountainside behind my tent and that came one by one to sing to us, to get acquainted, and to share our crumbs. Sometimes, in rainy weather, when the woods seemed wetter than the lake, Simmo would be sleeping philosophically and I reading or tying trout flies in the tent, and I would hear a gentle stir and a rustle under the tent fly. Then, if I crept out quietly, I might find Killooleet exploring my goods to find where the crackers grew, or just resting con-tentedly under the fly, where it was dry and comfortable.

It was good to live there among them, with the mountain at our backs and the lake at our feet and peace in every breeze. Rain or shine, day or night, these white-throated sparrows are the sunniest, cheeriest folk to be found anywhere in the woods. I grew to understand and love the Malecite name, Kil-looleet, Little Sweet-Voice, for its expressiveness. "Hour-Bird" the Micmacs call him, for they say he sings every hour to tell the time, "all same's one white man's watch." And indeed there is rarely an hour, day or night, in the northern woods when you cannot hear Killooleet singing. Other birds grow silent after they have won their mates, or they grow fat and lazy as summer advances, absorbed in the care of their young, and they have no time or thought for singing. But not so Killooleet. He is kinder to his mate after he has won her, and he never lets selfishness or the summer steal away his music, for he knows that the woods are brighter for his singing.

Sometimes, at night, I would take a brand from the fire and follow a deer path that wound about the mountain, or I would steal away into a dark thicket and strike a parlor match. As the flame shot up, lighting its little circle of waiting leaves, there would be a stir beside me in the underbrush or overhead in the fir. And tinkling out of the darkness, like a brook under the snow, would come the low clear strain of melody that always set my heart a-dancing—*I'm here, sweet Killooleet-lillooleet-lillooleet*—the good-night song of my gentle neighbor. Then along the path a little way and another match, and another song to make one better and his rest sweeter.

By day I used to listen to them, hours at a stretch, practicing to perfect their song. These were the younger birds, and for a long time they puzzled me. Those who know Killooleet's song will remember that it begins with three clear sweet notes, but very few have observed the break between the second and third of these. I noticed, first of all, that certain birds would start the song twenty times in succession, yet never get beyond the second note. And when I crept up to find out about it, I would find them sitting disconsolately, deep in shadow, instead of out in the light where they love to sing, with a pitiful little droop of wings and tail and the air of failure and dejection in every movement. Again, these same singers would touch the third note; and always, in such cases, they would prolong the last trill, the *lillooleet-lillooleet*, to an indefinite length instead of stopping at the second or third repetition, which is the rule with good singers. Then they would come out of the shadow, stir about briskly, and sing again with an air of triumph.

One day, while I was lying still in the underbrush watching a wood mouse, Killooleet, a fine male bird and a perfect singer, came and sang on a branch just over my head, not noticing me. Then I discovered that there is a trill, a tiny grace note or yodel, at the end of his second note. I listened carefully to other singers, as close as I could get, and found that it is always there, and it is the one difficult part of the song. You must be very close to the bird to appreciate the beauty of this little yodel; ten feet away it sounds like a faint *cluck* interrupting the flow of the third note, and a little farther away you cannot hear it at all.

Whatever its object, Killooleet regards this as the indispensable part of his song, and he never goes on to the third note unless he gets the second perfectly. That accounts for the many times one hears only the first two notes. That accounts also for the occasional prolonged trill, for when a young bird has tried his grace note many times without success and then gets it unexpectedly, he is so pleased with himself that he keeps up the final *lillooleet-lillooleet* as long as he has an atom of breath left to do it with.

But of all the Killooleets—and there were many that I soon recognized, either by their songs or by some peculiarity in their striped caps or brown jackets—the most interesting was the one who first perched on my ridgepole and bade me welcome to his camping ground. I soon learned to distinguish him easily: his cap was bright, his white cravat very full, and his song never stopped at the second note, for he had mastered the trill perfectly. Then, too, he was more friendly and fearless than all the others. The morning after our arrival we were eating breakfast by the fire, when he lit on the ground close by and turned his head sidewise to look at us curiously. I tossed him a big crumb, which made him run away in fright, but when he thought we were not looking he stole back, touched, tasted, ate the whole of it. When I threw him another crumb, he hopped to meet it.

After that he came regularly to meals. He would look critically over the tin plate which I placed at my feet and pick and choose daintily from the cracker and trout and bacon and porridge which I offered him. Soon he began to take bits away with him, and I could hear him, just inside the fringe of underbrush, persuading his mate to come and share his plate. But she was much shyer than he. It was several days before I noticed her flitting in and out of the shadowy underbrush, and when I tossed her the first crumb she flew away in a terrible fright. Gradually, however, Killooleet persuaded her that we were kindly, and she came often to meals; but she would never come near, to eat from my tin plate, until after I had gone away.

From then on never a day passed that one or both of the birds did not rest on my tent. When I put my head out in the early morning to look at the weather, Killooleet would look down from the projecting end of the ridgepole and sing good morning. When I had been out late on the lake, night fishing or following the inlet for beaver or watching the grassy points for caribou, I would listen with eager anticipation for Killooleet's welcome as I approached the landing. He had learned to recognize the sounds of my coming—the rub of a careless paddle, the ripple of water under the bow, or the grating of pebbles on the beach—and with Simmo asleep and the fire low, it was good to be welcomed back by a cheery little voice in the darkness, for he always sang when he heard me. Sometimes I would try to surprise him, but his sleep was too light and his ears too keen. The canoe would glide up to the old cedar and touch the shore noiselessly, but with the first crunch of gravel under my foot or the rub of my canoe as I lifted it over, he would waken; and his song, all sweetness and cheer, *I'm here, sweet Killooleet-lillooleet-lillooleet,* would ripple out of the dark underbrush where his nest was.

I am glad now to think that I never saw that nest, although it was scarcely ten yards from my tent, until after the young had flown and Killooleet cared no more about it. I knew in which bush it was, close by the deer path; I could pick out from my fireplace the thick branch that sheltered it, for I often watched the birds coming and going. I have no doubt that Killooleet would have welcomed me there without fear, but his mate never laid aside her shyness about it; she never went to it directly when I was looking, and I knew she would like me better if I respected her little secret.

Soon, from the mate's infrequent visits and from the amount of food which Killooleet took away with him, I knew she was brooding her eggs. And when, at last, both birds came together and, instead of helping themselves hungrily, each took the largest morsel he could carry and hurried away to the nest, I knew that the little ones had come. I spread the plate more liberally and moved it away to the foot of the old cedar, where Killooleet's mate would not be afraid to come at any time.

One day, not long after, as I sat at a late breakfast after the morning's fishing, there was a great stir in the underbrush. Presently Killooleet came skipping out, all fuss and feathers.

He ran back and forth with an air of immense importance between the last bush and the plate by the cedar, crying out in
his own way, "Here it is, here it is, all right, just by the old tree
as usual. Crackers, trout, brown bread, porridge; come on, come
on; don't be afraid. *He's* here, but he won't harm. I know him.
Come on, come on!"

Soon his little gray mate appeared, under the last bush,
and after much circumspection came hopping toward the breakfast. After her, in a long line, came five little Killooleets, hopping, fluttering, cheeping, stumbling—frightened at the big
world but in a desperate hurry for crackers and porridge. They
cast hungry eyes at the plate under the old cedar and stopped
briefly to turn their heads sidewise to see the big kind animal
that Killooleet had told them about, no doubt, many times.

After that we had often seven guests to breakfast, instead of
two. It was good to hear the lively *tink, tink-a-tink* of their
little bills on the tin plate in a merry tattoo, as I ate my own tea
and trout. I had only to raise my eyes to see them in a bobbing
brown ring about my bounty; and, just beyond them, the lap
of ripples on the beach, the lake glinting far away in the sunshine, and a bark canoe fretting at the landing, beckoning me
to come away as soon as I had finished my breakfast.

Before the little Killooleets had grown accustomed to things,
however, there occurred the most delicious bit of our summer
camping. It was only a day or two after their first appearance;
they knew simply that crumbs and a welcome awaited them at
my camp, but they had not yet learned that the tin plate in
the cedar roots was their special portion. Simmo had gone off
at daylight, looking up beaver signs for his fall trapping. I had
just returned from the morning fishing and was getting break-

fast, when I saw an otter come out into the lake from a cold brook over on the east shore. Grabbing a handful of figs and some pilot bread from the cracker box, I paddled away after the otter, for that is an animal which one has small chance to watch nowadays. Besides, I had found a den over near the brook, and I wanted to find out, if possible, how a mother otter teaches her young to swim.

I did not find out that day, because the young were already good swimmers. I watched the den for two or three hours from a good hiding place, and I got several glimpses of the mother and the little ones. On the way back I ran into a little bay, where a mother sheldrake was teaching her brood to dive and catch trout. Then I thought of a trap which Simmo had set two miles away, and I went to see if Nemox, the cunning fisher, who destroys the sable traps in winter, had been caught at his own game. So it was afternoon, and I was hungry, when I paddled back to camp. It occurred to me suddenly that Killooleet might be hungry, too, for I had neglected to feed him. He had grown sleek and comfortable of late, and he never went insect hunting when he could get cold fried trout and corn bread.

I landed silently and stole up to the tent to see if he were exploring under the fly, as he sometimes did when I was away. A curious sound, a hollow *tunk, tunk, tunk, tunk-a-tunk*, grew louder as I approached. I stole to the big cedar, where I could see the fireplace and the little opening before my tent, and I noticed first that I had left the cracker box open (it was almost empty) when I had hurried away after the otter. The curious sound was inside, growing more eager every moment—*tunk, tunk, tunk-a-trrrrrrunk, tunk, tunk!*

I crept on my hands and knees to the box to see what queer

thing had found his way to the crackers, and peeped cautiously over the edge. There were Killooleet, and Mrs. Killooleet, and the five little Killooleets, just seven hopping brown backs and bobbing heads, helping themselves to the crackers. And the sound of their bills on the empty box was the jolliest sound that ever came out of a camping kit.

I crept away more cautiously than I had come and, standing carelessly in my tent door, whistled the call I always used in feeding the birds. Like a flash Killooleet appeared on the edge of the cracker box, looking very much surprised. "I thought you were away; why, I thought you were away," he seemed to be saying. Then he clucked, and the *tunk-a-tunk* ceased instantly. Another cluck, and Mrs. Killooleet appeared, looking frightened. Then, one after another, the five little Killooleets bobbed up, and there they sat in a solemn row on the edge of the cracker box, turning their heads sidewise to see me better.

"There!" said Killooleet. "Didn't I tell you he wouldn't hurt you?" And like five winks the five little Killooleets were back in the box, and the tunk-a-tunking began again.

This assurance that they might do as they pleased and help themselves undisturbed to whatever they found seemed to re-move the last doubt from the mind of even the little gray mate. After that they stayed, most of the time, close about my tent, and they were never so far away or so busy insect hunting that they would not come when I whistled and scattered crumbs. The little Killooleets grew amazingly, and no wonder! They were always eating, always hungry. I took good pains to give them less than they wanted, and so I had the satisfaction of feeding them often and of finding their tin plate picked clean whenever I came back from fishing.

Did the woods seem lonely to Killooleet when we paddled away at last and left the wilderness for another year? That is a question which I would give much to answer. There is always a regret at leaving a good camping ground, but I had never packed up so unwillingly before. Killooleet was singing, cheery as ever, but my own heart was sad. Before leaving I had baked a loaf, big and hard, which I fastened with stakes at the foot of the old cedar; there was a tin plate under it and a bark roof above, so that when it rained and insects were hidden under the leaves, Killooleet and his little ones would find food and remember me. And so we paddled away and left them to the wilderness.

A year later my canoe touched the same old landing. For ten months I had been in the city, where Killooleet never sings and where the wilderness is only a memory. In the fall, on some long tramps, I had occasional glimpses of the little singer, solitary now and silent, stealing southward ahead of the winter. In the spring he showed himself rarely in the underbrush, on country roads, hurrying northward where the streams were clear and the big woods budding. But never a song in all that time; my ears were hungry for his voice as I leaped out to run eagerly to the big cedar. There were the stakes and the tin plate and the bark roof, all crushed by the snows of winter. The bread was gone; what Killooleet had spared, Tookhees the wood mouse had eaten thankfully. I found the old tent poles and put up my house leisurely, a hundred happy memories thronging about me. Suddenly there came a call, a clear whistle—and there he was, the same full cravat, the same bright cap, and the same perfect song to set my nerves a-tingling: *I'm here, sweet Killooleet-lillooleet-lillooleet!* And when I put crumbs by the old fireplace, he flew down to help himself, and went off with the biggest one, as of yore, to a new nest by the deer path.

Hukweem, the Night Voice

HUKWEEM, the loon, must go through the world crying for what he never gets and searching for one whom he never finds, for he is the hunting dog of Clote Scarpe. So said Simmo, my Indian guide, to me, one night, in explaining why the loon's cry is so wild and sad.

Clote Scarpe is a legendary hero, the Hiawatha of the northern Indians. Long ago he lived on the Wollastook and ruled the animals, which all lived peaceably together, understanding each other's language. But when Clote Scarpe went away they quarreled, and Lhoks, the panther, and Nemox, the fisher, took to killing the other animals. Malsun, the wolf, soon followed, and ate all he killed; and Meeko, the squirrel, who always makes all the mischief he can, set even the peaceable animals by the ears, so that they feared and distrusted each other. Then they scattered through the big woods, living each one for himself;

and now the strong ones kill the weak, and nobody understands anybody any more.

There were no dogs in those days. Hukweem was Clote Scarpe's hunting companion when he hunted the great evil beasts that disturbed the wilderness; and Hukweem alone, of all the birds and animals, remained true to his master. For hunting makes strong friendship, says Simmo; and that is true. Therefore does Hukweem go through the world, looking for his master and calling him to come back. Over the treetops, when he flies low looking for new waters; high in the air, out of sight, on his southern migrations; and on every lake, where he is only a voice, the sad night voice of the vast, solitary, unknown wilderness—everywhere you hear him seeking. Even on the seacoast, in winter, where he knows Clote Scarpe cannot be—for Clote Scarpe hates the sea—Hukweem forgets himself and cries occasionally out of pure loneliness.

When I asked what Hukweem says when he cries (for all cries of the wilderness have their interpretation) Simmo answered: "Wy, he say two ting. First he say, *Where are you? Oh, where are you?* Dass what you call his laugh, like he crazee. Denn, wen nobody answer, he say, *Oh, I so sorry, so sorry! Oo-ooo-eee!* like a woman lost in woods. An' dass his t'other cry."

This comes nearer to explaining the wild unearthliness of Hukweem's call than anything else I know. It makes things much simpler to understand, when you are camped deep in the wilderness, and the night falls, and out of the misty darkness under the farther shore comes a wild, shivering call that makes your nerves tingle. *Where are you? Oh, where are you?* That is just like Hukweem.

Sometimes, however, he varies the cry and asks very plainly: *Who are you? Oh, who are you?* On the Big Squattuk Lake,

where I camped one summer, there was a loon who was as full
of inquisitiveness as a blue jay. He lived alone at one end of the
lake, while his mate, with her brood of two, lived at the other
end, nine miles away. Every morning and evening he came
close to my camp—very much nearer than is usual, for loons are
wild and shy in the wilderness—to cry out his challenge. Once,
late at night, I flashed a lantern at the end of the old log that
served as a landing for the canoes, where I had heard strange
ripples; and there was Hukweem, examining everything with
the greatest curiosity.

Every unusual thing we did made him inquisitive. One time,
when I started down the lake with a fair wind and a small
spruce set up in the bow of my canoe for a sail, he followed me
four or five miles, calling all the way. And when I came back to
camp at twilight with a big bear in the canoe, his shaggy head
showing over the bow and his legs up over the middle thwart,
Hukweem's curiosity could stand it no longer. He swam up
within twenty yards and circled the canoe half a dozen times,
sitting up straight on his tail by a vigorous use of his wings,
stretching his neck like an inquisitive duck to look into the
canoe and see what queer thing I had brought with me.

He had another curious habit which afforded him unending
amusement. There was a deep bay on the west shore of the
lake, with hills rising abruptly on three sides. The echo here
was remarkable; a single shout brought a dozen distinct answers and then a confusion of tongues as the echoes and re-
echoes from many hills met and mingled.

One evening, as I was returning to camp from exploring the
upper lake, I heard a wild crying of loons on the west side.
There seemed to be five or six of the great divers, all laughing
and shrieking like lunatics. Pushing over to investigate, I no-

ticed for the first time the entrance to a great bay, and I paddled up cautiously behind a point to surprise the loons at their game. But when I looked in there was only one bird, Hukweem the Inquisitive. I knew him instantly by his great size and beautiful markings. He would give a single sharp call and listen intently, swinging his head from side to side as the separate echoes came ringing back from the hills. Then he would try his cackling laugh, *ooo-ah-ha-ha-ha-hoo! ooo-ah-ha-ha-ha-hoo!* and as the echoes began to clatter about his head he would get excited, sitting up on his tail, flapping his wings, cackling and shrieking with glee at his own performance. Every wild syllable was flung back like a shot from the surrounding hills, until the air seemed full of loons, all mingling their crazy cachinnations with the din of the chief performer. The uproar made one shiver. Then Hukweem would cease suddenly, listening intently to the warring echoes. Before the confusion was ended he would get excited again, and swim about in small circles, spreading wings and tail, showing his fine feathers as if every echo were an admiring loon, pleased as a peacock with himself at having made such a noise in a quiet world.

There was another loon, a mother bird, on a different lake, whose two eggs had been carried off by a thieving muskrat; but she did not know who did it. She came swimming down to meet us the moment our canoe entered the lake; and what she seemed to cry was, *Where are they? Oh, where are they?* as she followed us across the lake, accusing us of robbery and asking the same question over and over.

But whatever the meaning of Hukweem's crying, it seems to constitute a large part of his existence. Indeed, it is as a cry that he is chiefly known: the wild, unearthly cry of the wilderness night. His education for this begins very early. Once I was exploring the grassy shores of a wild lake when, out in the middle, a mother loon appeared suddenly with a great splashing and crying. I paddled out to see what was the matter. As I approached, she withdrew with apparently a great effort, still crying loudly and beating the water with her wings. I thought she had a nest in there somewhere and was trying to get me away from it, but this was the only time I had ever known a loon to try that old mother bird's trick. Generally they slip off the nest while the canoe is still half a mile away and swim under water a long distance, to watch you silently from the other side of the lake.

I went back and hunted awhile for the nest among the bogs of a little bay; then I left the search to investigate a strange call that sounded continuously farther up the shore. An eager little whistling cry came from a hidden spot in the tall grass, reminding me somehow of a nest of young fish hawks.

As I waded cautiously among the bogs, trying to locate the sound, I came suddenly upon the loon's nest—just a bare top of a bog, where the mother bird had pulled up the grass and hollowed the earth enough to keep the eggs from rolling out. They were there on the bare ground, two large olive eggs with dark blotches. I left them undisturbed and went on to investigate the crying, which had stopped the moment I approached the nest.

Presently it began again behind me, faint at first, then louder and more eager, until I traced it back to Hukweem's household. But there was nothing there to account for it, only two innocent-looking eggs on the top of a bog. I bent over to examine them more closely. There on the sides were two holes, and out of the holes projected the points of two tiny bills. Inside were two little loons, crying at the top of their lungs.

I left the work of release to the mother bird, thinking she knew more about it. But the next day I went back to the place and, after much watching, saw two little loons stealing in and out among the bogs, exulting in their freedom and silent as two shadows. The mother bird was off on the lake, fishing for their dinner.

Hukweem's fishing is always an interesting thing to watch. Unfortunately he is so shy that one seldom gets a good opportunity. Once I found his favorite fishing ground and came every day to watch him from a thicket on the shore. At my approach he would sink deeper into the water, as if taking in ballast. How he does this is a mystery, for his body is much lighter than its bulk of water. Dead or alive, it floats like a cork; yet without any perceptible effort he can sink it out of sight. Approach in a canoe and he moves off slowly, swinging his head from side to side to look at you, first with one eye, then with the other. Your canoe is swift; he sees that you are gaining; that you are already too near. He swings on the water and sits watching you steadily. Suddenly he begins to sink, deeper and deeper, until his back is just awash. Go a little nearer and his body disappears; only his neck and head remain above the water. Raise your hand, or make any quick motion, and he is gone altogether. He dives like a flash, swims deep and far, and when he comes to the surface he will be well out of danger.

If you notice the direction of his bill as it enters the water, you can tell fairly well where he will come up again. It was confusing at first, in chasing him, to find that he rarely came up where he was expected. I would paddle hard in the direction he was going, only to find him far to the right or left or behind me, when at last he showed himself. That was because I followed his body, not his bill. Moving in one direction, he will turn his head and dive. That is to mislead you, if you are following him. Follow his bill, as he does himself, and you will be near him when he rises, for he rarely turns under water.

With two good men to paddle, it is not difficult to tire him out. Although he swims with extraordinary rapidity under water —fast enough to follow and catch a trout—a long, deep dive tires him out, and he must rest before another. If you are chasing him, shout and wave your hat the moment he appears, and paddle hard the way his bill points as he dives again. The next time he comes up you are nearer to him. Send him down again quick, and after him. The next time he is frightened to see the canoe so close and dives deep, which tires him the more. So his disappearances become shorter and more confused. Suddenly he bursts out of the water beside you, scattering the spray into your canoe. Once he came up under my paddle, and I plucked a feather from his back before he got away.

This last appearance always scares him out of his wits, and you get what you have been working for: a sight of Hukweem getting under way. Off he goes in a smother of spray, beating the water with his wings, kicking hard to lift himself up; and so on for a hundred yards, leaving a wake like a stern-wheel steamer, until he gathers headway enough to rise from the water.

After that first start there is no sign of awkwardness. His short wings rise and fall with a rapidity that tires the eye to follow. You can hear the swift, strong beat of them, far over your head, when he is not calling. His flight is very rapid, very even, and often at enormous altitudes. But when he wants to come down he always gets frightened, thinking of his short wings, and how high he is, and how fast he is going. On the ocean, in winter, where he has all the room he wants, he sometimes comes down in a great incline, miles long, and plunges through and over a dozen waves, like a dolphin, before he can stop. But where the lake is small and he cannot come down that way, he has a dizzy time of it.

Once, on a little lake in September, I used to watch for hours to get a sight of the process. Twelve or fifteen loons were gathered there. They called down every migrating loon that passed that way, and their numbers increased daily. Twilight was the favorite time for arriving. In the stillness I would hear Hukweem far away, so high that he was only a voice. Presently I would see him whirling over the lake in a great circle. *Come down; oh, come down,* cried all the loons. *I'm afraid; ooo-ho-ho-ho-ho-hoooo-eee! I'm afraid,* said Hukweem, who was a little loon, all the way from Labrador on his first migration, and had never come down from a height before. *Come on; oh, come oh-ho-ho-ho-hon! It won't hurt you; come on,* cried all the loons.

Then Hukweem would slide down, lower with each circle, whirling round and round the lake in a great spiral, yelling all the time, with all the loons answering. When low enough, he would set his wings and plunge like a shot at the very midst of the assembly, which scattered wildly, yelling like schoolboys. So they splashed away in a desperate fright, each one looking back over his shoulder to see Hukweem come down, which he would do at a terrific pace, striking the water with a mighty splash and shooting half across the lake in a smother of white before he could get his legs under him and turn around. Then all the loons would gather around him, cackling, shrieking, laughing, with such a din as the little loon had never heard in his life before; and he would go off in the midst of them, telling them, no doubt, what a mighty thing it was to come down from so high and not break his neck.

Later in the fall I saw those same loons do an astonishing thing. For several evenings they had been keeping up an unusual racket in a quiet bay, out of sight of my camp. I asked Simmo what they were doing. "Oh, I don' know; playin' game, I guess, jus' like one boy. Hukweem do dat sometime, wen he not hongry," said Simmo, going on with his bean cooking. That excited my curiosity, but when I reached the bay it was too dark to see what they were playing.

One evening while I was fishing the racket was different from any I had heard before. There would be an interval of perfect silence, broken suddenly by wild yelling; then ordinary loon talk for a few minutes and another silence, broken by a shriller outcry. That meant that something unusual was going on, so I left the trout to find out about it.

When I pushed my canoe through the fringe of water grass on the point nearest the loons, they were scattered in a long line, twelve or fifteen of them, extending from the head of the bay to a point nearly opposite me. At the other end of the line two loons were swimming about, doing something which I could not make out. Suddenly the loon talk ceased. There may have been a signal given which I did not hear. Anyway, the two loons faced about at the same moment and came tearing down the line, using wings and feet to help in the race. The upper loons swung in behind them as they passed, to watch the finish better; but not a sound was heard until they passed my end of the line in a close, hard race, one scarcely a yard ahead of the other. Then such a yelling began as I never heard before. All the loons gathered about the two swimmers; there was much cackling and crying, which grew gradually quieter; then they began to string out in another long line, and two more racers took their places at one end of it. But that time it was almost dark, and I broke up the race trying to get nearer in my canoe.

Since then I have heard of two other people who have seen loons racing across a lake. I don't doubt it is a frequent pastime with the birds when the summer cares for the young are ended; autumn days are mellow, fish are plentiful, and there are long hours just for fun together, before Hukweem moves southward for the hard, solitary, winter life on the seacoast.

Of all the loons that cried out to me at night or shared the summer lakes with me, only one ever gave me the opportunity of watching at close quarters. It was on a very wild lake—so wild that no one had ever visited it before in summer—and a mother loon felt safe in leaving the open shore, where she generally nests, to place her eggs on a bog at the head of a narrow bay.

I used to go at all hours of the day, hoping the mother would get used to me and my canoe, so that I could watch her, later, teaching her little ones; but her wildness was unconquerable. Whenever I came in sight of the nest-bog, where only the loon's neck and head were visible, standing up straight and still in the grass, I would see her slip from the nest, steal away through the green cover to a deep place, and glide under water without leaving a ripple. Looking sharp over the gunwale into the clear water, I would get a glimpse of her—just a gray streak with a string of silver bubbles, passing deep and swift under my canoe.

So she went through the opening and appeared far out in the lake, where she would swim back and forth, as if fishing, until I went away. As I never disturbed her nest and always paddled away soon, she thought that she had fooled me and that I knew nothing about her or her nest.

Then I tried another plan. I lay down in my canoe, and had Simmo paddle me up to the nest. While the loon was out on the lake, hidden by the grassy shore, I went and sat on a bog, with a friendly alder bending over me, within twenty feet of the nest. Simmo paddled away, and Hukweem came back without the slightest suspicion. As I had supposed from the shape of the nest, she did not sit on her two eggs; she sat on the bog instead and gathered them close to her side with her wing. That was all the brooding they had or needed; for within a week there were two bright little loons to watch instead of the eggs.

After the first success I went alone and, while the mother bird was out on the lake, would pull my canoe up in the grass, a hundred yards or so below the nest. From here I entered the alders and made my way to the bog, where I could see Hukweem's household plainly. After a long wait she would steal into the bay, and, with much fear and circumspection, glide up to the canoe. It took a great deal of looking and listening to convince her that it was harmless and that I was not hiding near in the grass. Once assured, however, she would come direct to the nest, and I had the satisfaction at last of watching a loon at close quarters.

She would sit there for hours—never sleeping apparently, for her eye was always bright—preening herself, turning her head slowly to watch on all sides, snapping now and then at an obtrusive fly; all in utter unconsciousness that I was just behind her, watching every movement. When I had seen enough, I would steal away along a caribou path and push off quietly in my canoe without looking back. She saw me, of course, when I entered the canoe, but not once did she leave the nest. When I reached the open lake, a little searching with my glass always showed me her head there in the grass, still turned apprehensively in my direction.

I had hoped to watch her let the little ones out of their hard shell and to see them first take the water, but that was too much to expect. One day I heard them whistling in the eggs; the next day when I came there was nothing to be seen on the nest-bog. I feared that something had heard their whistling and put an untimely end to the young Hukweems while Mother Bird was away. But when she came back, after another fearful survey of the old bark canoe, two downy little fellows came bobbing to meet her out of the grass, where she had hidden them and told them to stay until she came back. Like all wild birds, she had carried the eggshells far away or swallowed them, lest their conspicuous whiteness guide some fierce, thieving eye to her household.

It was a rare treat to watch them at their first feeding; the little ones were all eagerness, bobbing about in the delight of eating and the wonder of the new great world, and the mother was all tenderness and watchfulness. Hukweem had never looked so noble to me before. This great wild mother bird moved ceaselessly with marvelous grace about her little ones, overseeing their play with exquisite fondness, watching the great dangerous world for their sakes, now chiding them gently, now drawing near to touch them with her strong bill or to rub their little cheeks with hers or just to croon over them in an ecstasy of wonderful mother love. In ten minutes she upset my theories and won me altogether, in spite of what I had heard and seen of her destructiveness on the fishing grounds. After all, why should she not fish as well as I?

Then began the first lessons in swimming and hiding and diving, which I had waited so long to see. I saw her bring little fish, which she had purposely crippled, turn them loose in shallow water, and with a sharp cluck bring the young loons out of their hiding to set them chasing and diving wildly for their own dinners. But before that happened there was almost a tragedy.

One day while the mother was gone fishing, the little ones came out of their hiding among the grasses and ventured out some distance into the bay. It was their first journey alone into the world; they were full of the wonder and importance of it. Suddenly, as I watched, they began to dart about wildly, moving with astonishing rapidity for such little fellows and whistling loudly. From the bank above, a swift ripple had cut out into the water between them and the only bit of bog with which they were familiar. Just behind the ripple were the sharp nose and beady eyes of Musquash, who is always in some mischief of this kind. In one of his prowlings he had discovered the little brood, and now he was maneuvering craftily to keep the frightened youngsters moving until they should be tired out, while he swam between them and the shore to cut off their retreat.

Musquash knows well that when a young loon or a black duck is caught in the open like that he always tries to get back where his mother hid him when she went away. That is what the poor little things were trying to do now, only to be driven back and kept moving wildly by the muskrat, who lifted himself occasionally from the water and wiggled his ugly jaws in anticipation of the feast. He had missed the eggs in his search, but young loons would be better. He snapped viciously, lunging at the nearest loon, which flashed under water and barely escaped.

I had started up to interfere, for I had grown fond of the little wild birds, when a great splashing began on my left and I saw the old mother bird coming like a fury. She was half swimming, half flying, tearing over the water at a great pace, a foamy white wake behind her. The little villain was going to get his medicine, I thought, and I dodged back to watch. Musquash, intent on his evil doing, kept on viciously after the exhausted little ones, paying no heed to his rear.

To my great astonishment, twenty yards away the mother bird flashed out of sight under the water. What could it mean! Suddenly a catapult seemed to strike the muskrat from beneath and lift him clear from the water. With a tremendous push and sputter Hukweem came out beneath him, her great pointed bill driven through to his spine. She had little need of my help now. With another straight hard drive, this time at eye and brain, she flung him aside disdainfully and rushed to her shivering little ones, questioning, chiding, praising them, all in the same breath, fluttering and cackling low in a hysteric wave of tenderness. Then she swam twice around the dead muskrat and led her brood away from the place.

Perhaps it was to one of those same little ones that I owe a service for which I am more than grateful. It was in September, and I was at a lake ten miles away. I was lost one day, hopelessly lost, trying to make my way from a trout pond where I had been fishing to the lake where my camp was. It was late afternoon. To avoid the long hard tramp down a river, up which I had come in the early morning, I had attempted to cut across through unbroken forest without a compass. Traveling through a northern forest in summer is desperately hard work. The moss is ankle deep, the underbrush is thick; fallen logs lie across each other in hopeless confusion, through and under and over which one must make his laborious way, stung and pestered by hordes of black flies and mosquitoes. Unless you have a strong sense of direction it is almost impossible to hold your course without a compass or a bright sun to guide you.

I had not gone half the distance before I was astray. The sun was obscured and a drizzling rain had set in, without any direction whatever in it by the time it reached the underbrush where I was. I had begun to make a little shelter, intending to put in a cheerless night there, when I heard a cry and, looking up, caught a glimpse of Hukweem speeding high over the tree-tops. Far down on my right came a faint answering cry, and I hastened in its direction. Hukweem was a young loon, and he was long in coming down. The crying ahead grew louder. Stirred up from their day rest by his arrival, the other loons began their sport earlier than usual. The crying soon became almost continuous, and I followed it straight to the lake.

Once there, it was a simple matter to find the river and my old canoe waiting patiently under the alders in the gathering twilight. Soon I was afloat again, with a sense of unspeakable relief. The loons were hallooing far away, and I went over— this time in pure gratitude—to see them again. But my guide was modest and vanished immediately into the group the moment my canoe appeared.

Since then, whenever I hear Hukweem in the night or hear others speak of his unearthly laughter, I think of that cry over the treetops and the thrilling answer far away. And the sound has a ring to it, in my ears, that it never had before. Hukweem the Night Voice found me astray in the woods and brought me safe to a snug camp. That is a service which one does not forget in the wilderness.

A *Fellow of Expedients*

THERE is among the birds one whose personal appearance is rapidly changing. He illustrates in his present life a process well known historically to all naturalists: the modification of form resulting from changed environment. I refer to the golden-winged woodpecker, perhaps the most beautifully marked bird of the North, whose names are as varied as his habits and accomplishments.

Nature intended him to get his living, as do other woodpeckers, by boring into old trees and stumps for the insects that live on the decaying wood. For this purpose she gave him the straight, sharp, wedge-shaped bill, just calculated for cutting out chips; the long, horn-tipped tongue for thrusting into the holes he makes; the peculiar arrangement of toes, two forward and two back; and the stiff, spiny tail feathers for supporting himself against the side of a tree as he works. But getting his living as nature intended means hard work, and he has discovered for himself a much easier way. Frequently now he is surprised on the ground in old pastures and orchards, floundering about rather awkwardly (for his little feet were never intended for walking) after the crickets and grasshoppers that abound there. Still he finds the work of catching them much easier than boring into dry old trees, and the insects themselves are much larger and more satisfactory.

A single glance will show how much this new way of living has changed him from the other woodpeckers. The bill is no longer straight, but has a decided curve like the thrush's; and instead of the chisel-shaped edge there is a rounded point. The red tuft on the head, which marks all the woodpecker family, would be too conspicuous on the ground. In its place we find a red crescent well down on the neck, partially hidden by the short gray feathers about it. The point of the tongue is less horny, and from the stiff points of the tail feathers laminae are beginning to grow, making them more like other birds'. A future generation will undoubtedly wonder where this peculiar kind of thrush got his unusual tongue and tail, just as we wonder at the deformed little feet and strange ways of a cuckoo.

The habits of this bird are a curious compound of his old life in the woods and his new preference for the open fields and farms. Sometimes the nest is in the very heart of the woods, where the bird glides in and out as silent as a crow in nesting time. His feeding place meanwhile may be an old pasture half a mile away, where he calls loudly and frolics about as if he had never a care or a fear in the world. But the nest is more frequently in a wild orchard, where the bird finds a knothole and digs down through the soft wood, making a deep nest with very little trouble. When the knothole is not well situated he finds a decayed limb and drills through the outer hard shell, then digs down a foot or more through the soft wood and makes a nest. In this nest the rain never troubles him, for he very providently drills the entrance on the underside of the limb.

Like many other birds, he has discovered that the farmer is his friend. Occasionally, therefore, he neglects to build a deep nest, simply hollowing out an old knothole and depending on the presence of man for protection from hawks and owls. At such times the bird soon learns to recognize those who belong in the orchard, and he loses the extreme shyness that characterizes him at all other times.

Once a farmer, knowing my interest in birds, invited me to come and see a golden-winged woodpecker which in her confidence had built so shallow a nest that she could be seen sitting on the eggs like a robin. The moment we crossed the wall, within sight of the nest, the bird slipped away out of the orchard. To test her, we withdrew and waited until she returned. Then the farmer passed within a few feet without disturbing her in the least. Ten minutes later I followed him, and the bird flew away again as I crossed the wall.

The notes of the golden-wing—much more varied and musical than those of other woodpeckers—are probably the results of his new free life and the modified tongue and bill. In the woods one seldom hears from him anything but a rattling tattoo, as he hammers away on a dry old pine stub. As a rule he seems to do this more for the noise it makes and the exercise of his abilities than because he expects to find insects (except in wintertime, when he goes back to his old ways). But out in the field he has a variety of notes. Sometimes it is a loud *kee-uk!*

like the scream of a blue jay divided into two syllables, with the accent on the last. At other times it is a cheery whistling call of very short notes run close together, with the accent on every other one. Or, occasionally, he teeters up and down on the end of a fence rail with a rollicking *eekoo, eekoo, eekoo* that sounds more like a laugh than anything else among the birds.

A curious habit which the bird has adopted with advancing civilization is that of providing himself with a sleeping place sheltered from the storms and cold of winter, instead of migrating to the South. Late in the fall he finds a deserted building, and after a great deal of shy inspection to satisfy himself that no one is within, drills a hole through the side. He has then a comfortable place to sleep and an abundance of decaying wood in which to hunt insects on stormy days. An icehouse is a favorite location for him; the warm sawdust furnishes a good burrowing place for a nest or sleeping room. When a building is used as a winter resort, the bird very cunningly drills the entrance close up under the eaves, where it is sheltered from storms and at the same time out of sight of all prying eyes.

During the winter several birds often occupy one building together. I know of one old deserted barn where five of the birds lived very peaceably together. At almost any hour of the day, if one approached cautiously and thumped the side of the barn, some of the birds would dash out in great alarm, never stopping to look behind them. At first there were only three entrances, but after I had surprised them a few times two more were added so they could get out more quickly when all were inside.

Two things about my family in the old barn aroused my

curiosity: what they were doing there by day, and how they got out so quickly when alarmed. The only way it seemed possible for them to dash out on the instant, as they did, was to fly straight through. But the holes were too small, and no bird but a bank swallow would have attempted such a thing.

One day I drove the birds out; then I crawled in under a sill on the opposite side and hid in a corner of the loft. It was a long wait in the stuffy old place before one of the birds came back. First I heard him light on the roof; then his little head appeared at one of the holes as he sat just below against the side of the barn, looking and listening before coming in. After a minute or two, quite satisfied that nobody was inside, he scrambled in and flew down to a corner where there was a lot of old hay and rubbish. Here he began a great rustle and stirring about, like a squirrel in autumn leaves; he was probably after insects, although it was too dark to see just what he was doing. It sounded part of the time as if he were scratching aside the hay, much as a hen would have done. If so, his two little front toes must have made sad work of it, with the two hind ones always getting doubled up in the way. When I thumped a board suddenly, he hurled himself like a shot at one of the holes, lighting just below it. I could hear plainly the thump of his little feet as he struck. With the same movement and without pausing an instant, he dived through headlong, aided by a spring from his tail. Hardly had he gone before another appeared, to go through the same program.

Although much shyer than other birds of the farm, the golden-winged woodpecker often ventures up close to the house in the early morning before anyone is stirring. One spring day I was awakened by a strange little pattering sound and, opening

my eyes, was astonished to see one of these birds on the sash
of the open window, within five feet of my hand. Half closing
my eyes, I kept very still and watched. Just in front of him, on
the bureau, was a stuffed golden-wing, with wings and tail
spread to show the beautiful plumage. Apparently this daring
one had seen it as he flew by, and now he stood hopping back
and forth along the window sash, uncertain whether to come
in or not. Sometimes he spread his wings, as if on the point of
flying in; then he would turn his head to look curiously at me
and at the strange surroundings, and endeavor to attract the
attention of the stuffed bird, whose head was turned away. In
the looking glass he saw his own movements repeated. Twice
he began his love call very softly, but cut it short as if frightened. The echo of the small room made it seem so different
from the same call in the open fields that I think he doubted
even his own voice.

Almost over his head, on a bracket against the wall, was a
great hawk, pitched forward on his perch, with wings spread
and fierce eyes glaring downward in the intense attitude a hawk
takes as he swoops for his prey. The golden-wing by this time
was ready to venture in. He had leaned forward with wings
spread, looking down at me to be quite sure I was harmless,
when, turning his head for a final look around, he caught sight
of the hawk just ready to pounce down on him. With a startled
kee-uk! he fairly tumbled back off the window sash, and I
caught one glimpse of him as he dashed round the corner in
full flight.

What were his impressions, I wonder, as he sat on a limb of
the old apple tree and thought it all over? What great wonders
he had seen! Did he have any means of communicating them
as he sang his love songs? What a wonderful story he could

tell, a real story, of a magic palace full of strangeness; of a glittering bit of air that made him see himself; of an enchanted beauty, stretching her wings in mute supplication for some brave knight to touch her and break the spell, while on high a fierce dragon-hawk kept watch, ready to eat up anyone who should dare enter!

And of course none of the birds would believe him. He would have to spend the rest of his life explaining, while the others would only whistle, and call him "Iagoo," the lying woodpecker. On the whole, perhaps it would be better for a bird with such a very unusual experience to keep still about it.

Kwaseekho

SHELDRAKE, or shelbird, is the name by which this duck is generally known. It was probably given to him by gunners, who see him only in winter when hunger drives him to eat mussels. The name fish duck, which one hears occasionally, is much more appropriate. His long slender bill, with serrated edges fitting into each other like the teeth of a bear trap, is just calculated to seize and hold a wriggling fish, and it is quite enough evidence as to the nature of the bird's food, even if one had not seen him fishing on the lakes and rivers which are his summer home.

That bill, by the way, is sometimes a source of danger. Once on the coast I saw a sheldrake trying in vain to fly against the wind, which flung him rudely among some tall reeds near me. The next moment Don, my old dog, had him. In a hungry moment the bird had driven his bill through both shells of a scallop, which had worked its way up to his nostrils, muzzling the bird perfectly with a hard shell ring. The poor fellow by desperate trying could open his mouth barely wide enough to drink or to swallow the tiniest morsel. He must have been in this condition a long time, for the bill was half worn through, and he was so light that the wind blew him about like a great feather when he attempted to fly.

Fortunately Don was a good retriever and had brought the duck in with scarcely a quill ruffled, so I had the satisfaction of breaking his bands and letting him go free with a splendid rush. But the wind was too much for him; he dropped back into the water and went skittering down the harbor. Meanwhile Don lay on the sand, head up, ears up, whining eagerly for the word to fetch. Then he dropped his head, and drew a long breath, and tried to puzzle it out why a man should go out on a freezing day in February to find a bird, only to let him go after he had been fairly caught.

Kwaseekho, the sheldrake, leads a double life. In winter he is found along the Massachusetts coast and southward, where he leads a dog's life, notwithstanding his gay appearance. A hundred guns roar at him wherever he goes. From daylight to dark he has never a minute to eat his bit of fish or to take a wink of sleep in peace. He flies to the ocean and beds with his fellows on the broad open shoals for safety. But the east winds blow, and the shoals are a yeasty mass of tumbling breakers. They buffet him about; they twist his gay feathers; they dampen his pinions, in spite of his skill in swimming. Then he goes to the creeks and harbors.

Along the shore a flock of his own kind, apparently, is feeding in quiet water. He comes straight in with unsuspecting soul, the morning light shining full on his white breast and bright red feet as he steadies himself to take the water. But *bang, bang!* go the guns, and out of a heap of seaweed come a man and a dog. And if he's lucky he goes away again, sadly puzzled at the painted decoys in the water.

Then the weather grows cold, and a freeze-up covers all his feeding grounds. Under his beautiful feathers the bones project to spoil the contour of his round plump body. He is famished; he watches the gulls to see what they eat. When he finds out, he forgets his caution and roams about after stray mussels on the beach. In the spring hunger drives him into the ponds, where food is plenty, but there the guns roar again. Altogether it is small wonder that, as soon as his instinct tells him the streams of the North are open and the trout running up, he is off to a land of happier memories.

In summer he forgets his hardships. His life is as peaceful as a meadow brook. His home is the wilderness—it may be on a lonely lake, shimmering under the summer sun, or perhaps it is a forest river, winding by wooded hills and grassy points and lonely cedar swamps. In secret shallow bays the young broods splash about, learning to swim and dive and hide in safety. The plunge of the fish hawk comes up from the pools. A noisy kingfisher rattles about from tree to stump like a restless busybody. The hum of insects fills the air with a drowsy murmur. Now a deer steps daintily down the point and looks, and listens, and drinks. A great moose wades awkwardly out to plunge his head under and pull away at the lily roots. But the young brood does not mind these harmless things. Sometimes, as the afternoon wears away, they turn their little heads apprehensively as the alders crash and sway on the bank above; a low cluck from the mother bird sends them all off into the grass to hide. But it is only a bear come down from the ridge where he has been sleeping to find a dead fish for his supper; and the little brood seems to laugh as another low cluck brings them scurrying back from their hiding.

Occasionally, there comes a real fright, when all the summer's practice is put to the test. An unusual noise is heard; and round the bend glides a bark canoe, with the sound of human voices. Away go the brood together, the river behind them foaming like the wake of a tiny steamer as the swift-moving feet lift them almost out of water. The poor mother flutters wildly about the brood, now leading, now bravely facing the monster, now pushing along some weak little loiterer, now floundering, as if wounded, near the canoe to attract attention from the young. But they double the point at last and hide away under the alders. The canoe glides by and makes no effort to find them. Silence is again over the forest. The little brood comes back to the shallows, with Mother Bird fluttering round them to count again and again, lest any be missing. The kingfisher comes out of his hole in the bank. The river flows on as before, and peace returns.

This is the way it all looks to me, sitting under a big hemlock, out of sight, and watching the birds through my field glass. Day after day I have attended their little schools, unseen and unsuspected by the mother bird. Sometimes it was the A B C class, wee little downy fellows, learning to hide on a lily pad and never getting their reward of a young trout until they hid so well that the teacher (somewhat overcritical, I thought) was satisfied. Sometimes it was the baccalaureates that displayed their talents, flashing out of sight, cutting through the water like a ray of light, striking a young trout on the bottom with almost the rapidity and certainty of the teacher. The diving

and swimming were marvelous, and Mother Bird looked on
and quacked her approval of the young graduates.

While all this careful training is going on at home, the drake
is off on the lakes somewhere with his boon companions, having a good time and utterly neglectful of parental responsibility. I have found clubs of five or six gay fellows, living by
themselves at one end of a big lake where the fishing was good.
All summer long they roam and gad about, free from care,
leaving the mother birds, meanwhile, to feed and educate their
offspring. Once only have I seen a drake sharing the responsi-
bilities of his family. I watched for three days to find the cause
of his devotion, but he disappeared the third evening and I
never saw him again. Whether the drakes are lazy and run
away, or whether they have the atrocious habit of many male
birds and animals of destroying their young and so are driven
away by the females, I have not been able to find out.

Occasionally one overtakes a brood on a rapid river. Then
the poor birds are distressed indeed. At the first glimpse of the
canoe they are off, churning the water into foam in their flight.
Not until they are out of sight around the bend do they hear
the cluck that tells them to hide. Some are slow in finding a
hiding place on the strange waters, but the mother bird hurries
them. They are hunting in frantic haste when round the bend
comes the swift-gliding canoe. With a note of alarm they are
all off again, for the mother will not leave even the weakest
alone. Again they double the bend and try to hide; again the
canoe overtakes them; and so on, mile after mile, until a stream
flowing into the river offers a road to escape. Then, like a flash,
the little ones run in under shelter of the overhanging banks
and glide upstream noiselessly, while the mother bird flutters
on down the river just ahead of the canoe. When she thinks she

has lured it away to a safe distance, she takes wing and returns
to the young.

Their powers of endurance are remarkable. Once, on the
Restigouche, we started a brood of little ones late in the afternoon. We were moving along in a good current, looking for a
camping ground, and had little thought for the birds, which
could never get far enough ahead to hide securely. For five
miles they kept ahead of us, rushing out at each successive
stretch of water and fairly distancing us in a straight run. When
we camped they were still below us. At dusk I was sitting motionless near the river when a slight movement by the opposite
bank attracted me. There was the mother bird, stealing along
upstream under the fringe of bushes. The young followed in
single file. There was no splashing of water now; no evidence
of fright or hurry. Shadows were not more noiseless.

Twice since then I have seen them do the same thing. I
have no doubt they returned that evening all the way back to
the feeding grounds where we first started them; for, like the
kingfishers, every bird seems to have his own piece of the
stream. He never fishes in his neighbor's pools, nor will he allow any poaching in his own. On the Restigouche we found a
brood every few miles; on other rivers, less plentifully stocked
with trout, they are less numerous. On lakes there is often a
brood at either end, but although I have watched them carefully, I have never seen them cross to each other's fishing
grounds.

Once, up on the Big Toledi, I saw a curious bit of their
education. I was paddling across the lake when I saw a shelbird
lead her brood into a little bay, where I knew the water was
shallow; immediately they began dipping, although very awkwardly. They were evidently taking their first lessons in diving.

The next afternoon I was near the same place. I had finished fishing and had pushed the canoe into some tall grass out of sight and was sitting there just doing nothing.

A musquash came by, rubbed his nose against the canoe, and nibbled a lily root before he noticed me. A shoal of minnows were playing among the grasses nearby. A deer stepped down the bank to drink and never saw me. Doing nothing pays under such circumstances, if only by the glimpses it gives of animal life. It is so rare to see a wild thing unself-conscious.

Then Kwaseekho came into the shallow bay again with her brood, and they began dipping as before. I wondered how the mother made them dive, until I looked through the field glass and saw that the little fellows occasionally brought up something to eat. There certainly were no fish to be caught in that warm, shallow water. But I had an idea, and I pushed the canoe out of the grass, sending the brood across the lake in wild confusion. There on the black bottom were a dozen young trout, all freshly caught, and all with the air-bladder punctures by the mother bird's sharp bill. She had provided their dinner, but she brought it to a good place and made them dive to get it.

As I paddled back to camp, I thought of the way the Indians taught their boys to shoot. They hung their dinner from the trees, out of reach, and made them cut the cord that held it with an arrow. Did the Indians originate this in their simple, direct way of looking at things? Or was the idea whispered to some Indian hunter long ago, as he watched Kwaseekho teach her young to dive?

Of all the broods I have met in the wilderness, only one, I think, ever grew to recognize me and my canoe a bit, so as to fear me less than another. I was on a little lake in the heart of the woods, where we lingered long on our journey, influenced by the beauty of the place. The brood was as wild as other broods; but I met them often, and without quite knowing how it came there they sometimes found the canoe lying motionless near them. So after a few days they looked at me with curiosity and uneasiness only, unless I came too near.

There were six in the brood. Five were hardy little fellows that made the water boil behind them as they scurried across the lake. But the sixth was a weakling. Perhaps he had been hurt by a hawk or a big trout or a mink; or maybe he was just a weak little fellow with no accounting for it. Whenever the brood was startled, he struggled bravely to keep up, but he always fell behind. The mother would come back to urge and help him, but it was of little use. He was not strong enough. The last glimpse I always had of them was a foamy wake disappearing round a distant point, while far astern was a ripple, where the little fellow still paddled away, pathetically doing his best.

One afternoon the canoe glided round a point and ran almost up to the brood before they saw it, giving them a terrible fright. Away they went on the instant, lifting themselves almost out of water with the swift-moving feet and tiny wings. The mother bird took wing, returned, and crossed the bow of the canoe, back and forth, with loud quackings. The weakling was behind as usual, and in a sudden spirit of curiosity I shot the canoe forward, almost up to him. He tried to dive, got tangled in a lily stem in his fright, came up, flashed under again; and I saw him rise to the surface, ten feet away, in some grass, where he sat motionless and almost invisible amid the pads and yellow stems. How frightened he was, yet how still he sat! Whenever I took my eyes from him a moment I had to hunt again, sometimes two or three minutes, before I could

see him there. But I remained where I was to watch him and
see what the mother would do.

Meanwhile the brood went almost to the opposite shore before they stopped; the mother, satisfied at last by my quietness,
flew over and lit among them. She had not seen the little one.
Through the glass I saw her flutter round and round them, to
be quite sure they were all there. Then she missed him. She
must have clucked, I think, for the young suddenly disappeared
and she came swimming rapidly back over the way they had
come, looking, looking everywhere. She went around the canoe
at a safe distance, searching among the grass and lily pads, calling him softly to come out. But he was very near the canoe
and very much frightened; the only effect of her calls was to
make him crouch closer against the grass stems, while the
bright little eyes, grown large with fear, were fastened on me.

Slowly I backed the canoe away until it was out of sight
behind the point, although I could still see the mother bird
through the bushes. She swam rapidly about where the canoe
had been, calling more loudly, but the little fellow was too
frightened and refused to show himself. At last she discovered
him and, with quacks and flutters that looked to me a bit
hysterical, pulled him out of his hiding place. How she fussed
over him! She hurried and helped and praised and scolded him
all the way over; she fluttered on ahead and clucked the brood
out of their hiding places to meet him! Then, with all her
young about her, she swept round the point into the quiet bay.

And I, drifting slowly up the lake into the sunset, was thinking how human it all was. "Doth he not leave the ninety and
nine in the wilderness, and go after that which is lost, until
he find it?"

Koskomenos, the Outcast

KOSKOMENOS, the kingfisher, is an outcast among the birds. I think they regard him as a half reptile who has not yet climbed high enough in the bird scale to deserve recognition, so they let him severely alone. Even the goshawk hesitates before taking a swoop at him, not knowing whether the gaudy creature is dangerous or only uncanny. I saw a great hawk once drop like a bolt upon a kingfisher that hung on quivering wings, rattling softly, before his hole in the bank. But the robber lost his nerve at the instant when he should have dropped his claws to strike. He swerved aside and shot upward in a great slant to a dead spruce top, where he stood watching intently until the dark beak of a brooding kingfisher reached out of the hole to receive the fish that her mate had brought her. Then Koskomenos swept away to his watchtower above the minnow pool, and the hawk set his wings toward the outlet, where a brood of young sheldrakes were taking their first lessons in the open water.

No wonder the birds look askance at Kingfisher. His head is ridiculously large; his feet are ridiculously small. He is a poem of grace in the air, but he creeps like a lizard or waddles like a duck in the rare moments when he is afoot. His mouth is big enough to take in a minnow whole; his tongue is so small that he has no voice and can only make a harsh *klr-r-r-r-ik-ik-ik-ik*, like a watchman's rattle. He builds no nest, but has a den in a bank, where he lives most filthily half of the day; yet the other half he is a clean, beautiful creature, whose bright garments have no suggestion of earth but only reflect the blue heavens above and the color-steeped lake below. Water will not wet him, although he plunges a dozen times beneath the surface. His clatter is harsh, noisy, diabolical; but his plunge into the stream, a flash of color and silver spray and the tinkle of smitten water, is the most musical thing in the wilderness.

As a fisherman he has no equal. His fishy, expressionless eye is the keenest that sweeps the water, and his swoop puts even the fish hawk to shame for its certainty and its lightning quickness.

But he is solitary, unknown, inapproachable. He has no youth, no play, no joy except to eat; he associates with nobody, not even with his own kind. And when he catches a fish, and beats it against a limb until it is dead, and sits with his head tilted back, swallowing his prey, with a clattering chuckle deep down in his throat, a suspicion creeps over you, as you watch, that the birds are right in casting him out; that there is too much lizard still left in him to class him properly among the fowls of the air.

It is this strange mixture of bird and reptile that has made the kingfisher an object of superstition among savage peoples. The legends about him are legion; his crested head is prized above all others by savages as a charm or fetish; and even among civilized people his dried body may still sometimes be seen hanging to a pole, in the belief that his bill will point out the quarter from which the next wind will blow.

But Koskomenos has another side, although the world, as yet, has found out little about it. One day in the wilderness I cheered him quite involuntarily. It was late afternoon; the fishing was over, and I sat in my canoe watching for anything that might come along. Across the stream was a clay bank, near the top of which a dark hole showed where a pair of kingfishers had dug their long tunnel. "There is nothing for them to stand on there; how did they begin that hole?" I wondered lazily; "and how can they ever raise a brood, with an open door like that for mink and weasel to enter?"

A movement under the shore stopped my wondering, and the long lithe form of a hunting mink stole swiftly upstream. He stopped under the hole, raised himself with his fore paws against the bank, twisting his head from side to side and sniffing nervously. Then he began to climb. But the bank was sheer and soft; he slipped back half a dozen times without rising two feet. So he went downstream to a point where some roots gave him a foothold, and he ran lightly up until he was under the dark eaves that threw their shadows over the clay bank. There he crept cautiously along until his nose found the nest, when he slipped down and rested his fore paws on the threshold. He took a long sniff of the rank fishy odor that pours out of a kingfisher's den and a keen look all around to be sure the old birds were not returning; then he vanished like a shadow.

I thought that was the end of one brood of kingfishers, but scarcely was the thought formed when a fierce rumbling clatter sounded in the bank. The mink shot out, a streak of red showing plainly across his brown face. After him came a kingfisher, clattering out a storm of invectives and aiding his progress by vicious jabs at his rear. He had made a miscalculation that time; the old mother bird was at home waiting for him, and she drove her powerful beak at his evil eye the moment it appeared at the inner end of the tunnel. That took the longing for young kingfisher all out of Cheokhes. He plunged headlong down the bank, the bird swooping after him with a rattling alarm that brought another kingfisher in a twinkling. The mink dived, but it was useless to attempt escape that way; the keen eyes above followed his route perfectly. When he came to the surface, twenty feet away, both birds were over and dropped like plummets on his head. So they drove him downstream and out of sight.

Years afterward I solved the second problem suggested by the kingfisher's den when I had the good fortune one day to watch a pair beginning their tunneling. All who have ever watched the bird have no doubt noticed his wonderful ability to stop short in swift flight and hold himself poised in midair for an indefinite time while watching the movements of a minnow beneath. They make use of this ability in beginning their nest on a bank so steep as to afford no foothold.

As I watched this pair, first one and then the other would hover before the point selected, as a hummingbird balances for a moment at the opening of a trumpet flower. Then the kingfisher drove his beak with rapid plunges into the bank, sending down a continuous shower of clay to the river below. In a remarkably short time they had a foothold and proceeded to dig themselves in out of sight.

Kingfisher's tunnel is so narrow that he cannot turn around in it. His straight, strong bill loosens the earth; his tiny feet throw it out behind. I would see a shower of dirt and perhaps the tail of Koskomenos for a brief instant, then a period of waiting and another shower. This kept up until the tunnel was bored in about two feet, when it is their custom to make a sharp turn. After that they brought most of the earth out in their beaks. While one worked, the other watched or fished at the minnow pool, so that there was steady progress as long as I observed them.

A curious thing about these birds, which you may see for yourself on any wilderness river, is that each pair of kingfishers have their own particular pools, over which they exercise un-questioned lordship. There may be a dozen pairs of birds on a single stream; but, as far as I have been able to observe, each family has a certain stretch of water on which no other king-fishers are allowed to fish. They may pass up and down freely, but they never stop at the minnow pools; if they are caught watching near them, they are promptly driven out by the right-ful owners. The same thing is true on lake shores. But whether there is some secret understanding and partition among them, or whether their rights consist in discovery or first arrival, there is no means of knowing.

I had not half settled this matter of the division of trout streams when I discovered another utterly unexpected aspect of the kingfisher. Koskomenos, half reptile though he may be, not only recognizes riparian rights, but he is also capable of friendship even if he is a moody prowler of the wilderness whom no one else cares about.

I was out in my canoe alone one midsummer day, looking for a loon's nest, when the fresh tracks of a bull caribou drew me to the shore. The trail led straight from the water to a broad alder belt, beyond which, on the hillside, I hoped to find the big brute loafing his time away until evening came.

As I turned shoreward, a kingfisher sounded his rattle and came darting across the mouth of the bay. I watched him, admiring the rippling sweep of his flight, like the run of a cat's-paw breeze across a sleeping lake, and the clear blue of his crest against the deeper blue of summer sky. Opposite my canoe he checked himself, poised an instant in mid-air, watching the minnows that my paddle had disturbed, and dropped bill first. A shower of spray caught the rainbow for a brief instant; the ripples gathered over the spot where Koskomenos had gone down, when they were scattered rudely again as he burst out among them with his fish. He swept back to the stub from which he had come, chuckling on the way. There he whacked his fish soundly on the wood, threw his head back, and through the glass I saw the tail of a minnow wriggling slowly down his throat. Then I took up the caribou trail.

I had gone nearly through the alders, following the course of a little brook, when behind me I heard the kingfisher coming above the alders, rattling as if possessed, *klrrr! klrrr! klrrr-ik-ik-ik!* At the same moment there was a heavy plunge and splash just ahead, and the swift rush of some large animal up the hillside. The kingfisher poised over me, looking down first at me, then ahead at the unknown beast, until the crashing ceased in a faint rustle far away. Then the bird swept back to his fishing stub, clacking and chuckling immoderately.

I pushed cautiously ahead and came presently to a beautiful pool, below a rock, where the hillside shelved gently toward the alders. From the numerous tracks and the look of the place I knew instantly that I had stumbled upon a bear's bathing pool. The water was still troubled; huge tracks, all soppy and broken, led up the hillside in big jumps; the moss was torn, the underbrush spattered with shining waterdrops. Obviously, Mooween had been asleep in this pool and the kingfisher woke him up. But why? Did he do it on purpose? And I began to wonder how the rattle of a kingfisher, which is one of the commonest sounds on lonely waters, could scare a bear, who knows all the sounds of the wilderness perfectly.

Perhaps Koskomenos has an alarm note and uses it for a friend in time of need, as gulls go out of their way to warn a flock of sleeping ducks when danger is approaching. Here was a new trait, a touch of the human in this unknown, clattering suspect of the fishing stream. I resolved to watch him with keener interest.

Somewhere above me, deep in the tangle of the summer wilderness, Mooween stood watching, eyes, ears, and nose alert to discover what the creature was who dared frighten him out of his noonday bath. It would be senseless to attempt to surprise him now; so I marked the place and stole away to my canoe.

But the next day when I came back, creeping quietly along the upper edge of the alders, the pool was clear and still, as if nothing but the little trout had ever disturbed its peace. Koskomenos was clattering about the bay below, as usual. In spite of my precautions he had seen me enter the alders, but he paid no attention to me whatever. He went on with his fish-

ing as if he knew perfectly well that the bear had deserted the
bathing pool.

It was nearly a month before I again camped on the beautiful
lake. Summer was gone. Here and there birches and maples
flung out their gorgeous banners of autumn over the silent water. A tingle came into the evening air; the lake's mist lay heavy
and white in the twilight stillness; birds and beasts became
suddenly changed as they entered the brief period of sport and
full feeding.

I was drifting about the same reedy bay, shooting frogs for
my table with a pocket rifle. This was very different from
the woods about my home. There the game was already
harried; the report of a gun set every living creature skulking.
Here the crack of my little rifle was no more heeded than the
plunge of a fish hawk or the groaning of a burdened elm bough.
A score of fat woodcocks lay unheeding in a bit of alder tangle;
when I appeared upon the burned hillside the partridges
jumped to a tree and craned their necks to see what I was. The
black ducks skulked in the reeds. They were full-grown now
and strong of wing, but the early hiding habit was not yet
broken by shooting. The mink, changing from brown to black,
gave up his nest robbing for honest hunting, undismayed by
trap or deadfall; and, up in the inlet, I could see grassy domes
rising above the bronze and gold of the marsh, where the beavers were building thick and high for winter cold and spring
floods. Truly it was good to be here and to enter for a brief
hour into the shy, wild life of the wood folk.

Then there was a sudden movement in the alders on the
shore. At the same moment a kingfisher went rattling by to his
old perch over the minnow pool. The alders swayed again as if

struck, and a huge bear lumbered out of them to the shore with a disgruntled *woof!* at some twig that had switched his ear too sharply.

I slid lower in the canoe until only my head and shoulders were visible. Mooween went nosing alongshore until something touched his appetite, when he stopped and began feeding, scarcely two hundred yards away. I reached first for my heavy rifle, then for the paddle, and cautiously fanned the canoe toward shore up to an old stump which covered my approach. But I had scarcely started forward when over my head swept Koskomenos with a rush of wings and an alarm cry that spoke only of haste and danger. I had a glimpse of the bear plunging into the alders, while the kingfisher wheeled in a great rattling circle about the canoe before he pitched upon the old stump, jerking his tail and clattering in great excitement.

I swung noiselessly out into the lake, where I could watch the alders. They were all still for a space of ten minutes; but I knew Mooween was there, sniffing and listening. Then a great snake seemed to be wriggling through the bushes, making no sound but showing a wavy line of quivering tops as he went.

A little way down the shore was a higher point, with a fallen tree that commanded a view of half the lake. Mooween evidently knew the spot; the alders showed that he was heading straight for it, to look out on the lake and see what the alarm was about. As yet he had no idea what peril had threatened him, but, like all wild creatures, he had obeyed the first clang of a danger note on the instant. There is not a creature in the woods, from Mooween down to Tookhees, the wood mouse, who has not learned from experience that, in matters of this kind, it is well to jump to cover first and investigate afterwards.

I paddled swiftly to the point, landed, and crept to a rock

from which I could just see the fallen tree. Mooween was coming. I thought he was surely my bear this time. Then Koskomenos swept into the woods, hovering over the brush, looking down and rattling—*klrrr-ik, clear out! klrrr-ik, clear out!* There was a heavy rustle, as a bear always makes when he is alarmed; Koskomenos swept back to his perch; and I sought the shore, half inclined to make my next hunting more even-chanced by disposing of one meddlesome factor.

The front sight of my rifle rested fair on the blue back of Koskomenos, but slowly the bent finger relaxed on the trigger. A loon went floating by the point, all unconscious of danger. Far overhead soared an eagle, looking down on his own wide domain, unheeding the man's intrusion. Nearer, a red squirrel barked down his resentment from a giant spruce trunk. On my left a heavy splash and a wild, free tumult of quacking told where the black ducks were coming in, as they had done, undisturbed, for generations. Behind me a long roll of a young cock partridge echoed through the woods, and from the mountainside a cow moose rolled back a startling answer. Close at hand, a chipmunk was chunking sleepily in the sunshine; a nest of young wood mice were calling their mother in the grass at my feet. And every wild sound did but deepen the vast, wondrous silence of the wilderness.

The roar of a rifle had no place in this blessed peace, I told myself sadly. As if in answer, the kingfisher dropped with his musical splash and swept back with exultant rattle to his watchtower. And I went to the point to measure the tracks, to estimate how big the bear was, and to console myself with the thought of how I would certainly have had him—if something had not interfered.

A few days later the chance came to repay Koskomenos with coals of fire. The lake surface was still warm; no storms nor frosts had cooled it. The big trout had risen from the deep places, but they were not yet quickened enough to take my flies; so, trout hungry, I was trolling for them with a minnow. I had taken two good fish and was moving slowly by the mouth of the bay, Simmo at the paddle, when a suspicious movement on the shore line attracted my attention. I passed the line to Simmo, the better to use my glasses, and was scanning the alders sharply, when a cry of wonder came from the Indian. And there, twenty feet above the lake, a young kingfisher—one of the Koskomenos' frowzy-headed, wild-eyed youngsters—was whirling wildly at the end of my line. He had seen the minnow trailing a hundred feet astern and, with more hunger than discretion, had swooped for it promptly. Simmo, feeling the tug but seeing nothing behind him, had struck promptly, and the hook went home.

I seized the line and began to pull in gently. The young kingfisher came most unwillingly, with a continuous chatter of protest that speedily brought Koskomenos and his mate and two or three of the captive's brethren. They showed no lack of courage, but swooped again and again at the line and even at the man who held it. In a moment I had the youngster in my hand, and I disengaged the hook. He was not hurt at all, but terribly frightened; so I held him a little while, enjoying the excitement of the others, whom the captive's rattle kept circling wildly about the canoe. It was noteworthy that not another bird heeded the cry or came near. Even in distress they refused to recognize the outcast. Then, as Koskomenos hovered on quivering wings just over my head, I tossed the captive close up beside him.

But there was no note of gratitude in the noisy babel that swept up the bay after the kingfishers. When I saw them again, they were sitting on a dead branch, five of them in a row, chuckling and clattering all at once, unmindful of the minnows that played beneath them. I have no doubt that, in their own way, they were telling each other all about it.

Pheasant Lore

MY acquaintance with the ringneck pheasant dates back to his first appearance in my part of the country. It was many years ago in a Connecticut township of scattered farms and excellent covers where, unknown to me, a local sportsman had released a variety of imported game on his own land for his own pleasure. Going there on a grouse hunt one November morning, I let my setter Rab limber his legs in an open field before entering the nearest good cover. He was quartering his ground at speed when he whirled to a half point, held it a moment, and trailed away on a hot scent, his nose in the air.

Thinking that a grouse might have pitched down in the open, I followed the setter with an occasional low-voiced *whoa* that checked him long enough for me to keep within shooting distance. Across the field he trailed, into and through an alder swale, up a bare hillside, through a wood lot, over a fence into an abandoned pasture upgrown to weeds and brush, where I lost sight of him. By that time I was wondering what he was trailing. Certainly it was not a grouse. When found again he was steadily pointing a thicket so choked by cat briers that only a cottontail would feel at home there.

I was forcing a way into the tangle, one arm shielding my face, when the earth exploded underfoot. Something like a yard-long rocket towered up, up, up, with a heathenish cackle that sounded like a curse on dogs and men. At the shot Rab broke point for the first time in years, whipping around the tangle as if bent on catching the game as it fell. And he almost did it. Back he came, with wagging plume, feeling immensely proud of himself, as well he might feel after such perfect work. That was the first cock pheasant I had ever seen or heard.

At that time the planting of pheasants was regarded in New England as a very doubtful experiment. Believing that it was worth trying, if only to relieve the increasing pressure on our native game birds, I started by raising a few broods from the egg and releasing them in covers of my own selection. For the next seventeen years it was my good luck to observe a score or more wild pheasants that came daily from November to April to feed at one of the "bird tables" in my back yard. And on a game farm where thousands of pheasants were raised every season it interested me to note their behavior pattern from tiny chicks under an electric brooder to grown birds that went off in crates by the truckload. During every open season, meanwhile, it was a satisfaction to find that they were certainly taking a lot of pressure from quail, grouse, and woodcock. Of every ten hunters I met afield, eight or nine were chasing over the countryside with their dogs in the hope of bagging a ringneck.

After the long association I must sadly record that there are only two places where a cock pheasant looks good to me: in full autumn plumage over my gun sight, and nicely browned on my dining table. At all other times he is an outlandish bird, gaudy colored, raucous voiced; his head, with its ugly red-check patches and feathered horn, reminds me of the grotesque creatures carved by degenerate Indian tribes on their totem poles. As for his inner character, if he has any gentle or lovable quality, it is never displayed. He alternately bullies and neglects his mate, drives his offspring away from food, and treats other cocks with indifference except during the mating season, when he meets them with the ferocity of a game rooster bent on a killing.

One springtime morning, while we were driving slowly through the country, my little daughter exclaimed, "Look, Daddy, look! Two lovely pheasants, just like those in our yard at home." On a bare brown field two cocks were crouched close to earth, their heads moving jerkily up-down, up-down in perfect unison, as if moved by the same clock spring. One would lift his head with intent to jump on the other's back; the other, watching his opponent's eye and seeing there the action before it started, would jerk up his head to an equal level. At the same instant both leaped into the air, each driving his beak at the other's eye and his spurs into the other's body.

Having seen the beginning of such a duel I might, if left to myself, have watched to see how this one ended, but there was only one answer to a distressed little voice saying, "Oh, they're fighting, Daddy. Please stop them." So over the fence I went to play the role of peacemaker, which was the last thing the cocks wanted. Scattered feathers and glistening drops of blood showed that they had been fighting a long while, so bedeviled by a hateful lust to kill that I came within arm's reach before they took to wing. Flying heavily, one close behind the other, they crossed the field and dropped from sight under a wall. Both were as near a knockout as any bird could be and keep his feet, yet when I looked over the wall they were at it again. This time I clouted them apart with my hat, driving them in opposite directions to make sure that they would not carry on their fight until one or both were food for the beetle. What a better ending it might be, I thought, for some lucky sportsman to see them over his gun sight as they cackled up from a pointing dog.

Among the ringneck's outstanding qualities I should place, first of all, his utter wildness. Whether hand-raised on a farm or hen-raised on a huckleberry hill, he is the same untamable bird. Even the pheasants that fed at my table regarded me suspiciously; never for a moment would they trust me or any of my kind. Many a morning I kept them waiting a hungry hour, hoping they might welcome my coming. Native birds that fed from a table nearer the house would come to my call; if I were late, they would flutter at the window to remind me that it was breakfast time. But the pheasants would not show themselves so long as I was within their sight range. On a morning after a storm, when they were searching for food around the snow-covered table and I approached, scattering grain or giving the food call, they would all wink away into hiding—as wild after a six-month acquaintance as they were the first day.

On a game farm, where strangers are taboo, the keeper may enter a big holding pen without greatly alarming the pheasants; but even here, their wildness often has a lunatic streak in it. More than once, at the drowsy midday hour, I have sat quiet and unseen beside a holding pen of well-grown birds, all hidden in the dense ground cover. Nothing might stir for an hour or two; then without warning would come a squawk of alarm. Another squawk would answer like an echo, and with a thunderous roar of wings accompanied by crazy cackling a hundred pheasants would be knocking their heads against the woven-wire ceiling in a frenzy of senseless excitement. The clamor would end as suddenly and as mysteriously as it began.

Many of these pheasants are used by the owner to stock a private shooting preserve, into which he may release forty or fifty strong-flying birds at a time. And the reason they stay within bounds instead of scattering over the countryside is amazingly simple. On the preserve are three small holding pens, open at the top, with sides high enough to prevent a pinioned bird from jumping out. Each pen holds a dozen or more pheasants that are always well fed and watered. At sundown most of the free birds gather around one or other of the holding pens, and some of them, as I have repeatedly proved, fly into the pen to spend the night. A possible explanation is that the artificial habit of crowding is so fixed upon the chicks that they follow it when they would be much safer from predators if they scattered widely for the night.

Pheasants bred naturally in the wild have a bedding habit that is more interesting because it is apparently a matter of choice. When the chicks are small the hen leads them to the best feeding or loafing place by day; at sundown she leads them under a dense cover of dead weeds or into a bramble patch or, best of all, a field upgrown to goldenrod with stems so thickly crowded that even the blacksnake avoids it. Such care, so far as can be observed, is all that a hen pheasant ever gives to her young toughies. A mother quail or a mother grouse will risk her life by fluttering around an enemy, holding his attention while her chicks escape; but I have never seen a hen pheasant do anything but run away or fly away from danger, leaving her chicks to look out for themselves. When well grown the brood, singly or in small groups, heads at sundown for the nearest bog or swamp. For the greater part of the distance they travel on their legs, but when within forty yards of the swamp they take to wing and drop into their scattered bedrooms from the air.

Of several places where I have observed pheasants come home to roost the most rewarding was a lonely twenty-acre swamp. Around it grew a fringe of high-bush blueberries; its gloomy heart was marshland with a few brushy hillocks and a myriad tussocks of saw grass separated by stagnant water. There are two answers, both natural and therefore reasonable, to why pheasants sleep in such an unlikely place. A night prowler such as a fox or cat rarely enters swampy ground, being unwilling to wade in water; and by dropping into it from the air, the pheasant leaves no trail for other enemies to follow. Whether they act intelligently or by instinct is a question for endless argument and futile waste of opinions, since only a pheasant knows the answer. In this connection, the one thing of which most sportsmen are convinced is that an old cock knows well what he is doing and why: Take for example his uncanny ability to hide his gaudy-colored bulk where a robin could be seen as plainly as a fish in a glass bowl.

One day I got an invitation to go out with a man who likes to hunt pheasants with his cocker spaniel. Because his hunting ground was new to me, I accepted his invitation on two conditions: that I be free to look into any grouse or woodcock cover, and that my setter be left at home. The cocker is a lovely little dog but no fit bracemate for a pointing dog. I was near a rail fence in an open field when from the other side of a ridge came the faint report of my comrade's twenty-gauge. A minute later a cock pheasant flamed into sight, sunlight gleaming from his burnished coat, coming nearer on a long downward slant until he pitched beside a fence post.

Marking the spot, I walked in, telling myself, "That bird is as good as in the bag." Not a living thing was in sight where, it seemed, a sparrow must be plainly visible. Thinking that the cock had sneaked along the fence under the lowest rail, I walked to the end of it, some sixty yards distant. The moment I turned back, up flared the cock, *kak-kak-kak*, from the very post where I had marked him down. On one side of the post was a rain-washed hole no bigger than my cap; in it, helped by a tuft of unmown grass, the cock had hidden long enough to rest his wings for a flight to the nearest cover.

Another time, a week before the shooting season opened, I was training two setter pups to quarter their ground in an open field. On one side were houses beside a road; on the other side was the only cover in sight. From one end of the field the pups were waved off in opposite directions; on coming to the edge they were waved to the other side (a method which covers the ground in half the time the pups would cover it in their own helter-skelter way). To my surprise, for no game was expected, one pup caught a scent and was trailing it when he locked up on point. The other pup was angling toward him at a fast clip when he, too, locked up, either because he had caught a body scent or was honoring his bracemate's point, as good dogs do.

Between the pointing pups my eye could detect nothing to break the level except a tiny, formless hump. With my attention fixed on that hump I moved in, thinking to find a box tortoise, which has a gamy smell that some dogs like. I was within a dozen feet when by some incredible magic the tiny hump turned itself into a cock pheasant. He had been running to cover from one enemy when he almost bumped into another that blocked his way of escape. On the instant he had flattened out close to earth, motionless from outstretched neck to the tip of his long tail. The only thing that camouflaged his outline was a tuft of grass that had grown around a dried cow pad. When to test the pups' steadiness I half circled the cock, he never moved a feather; only his eye, bright as a jewel, told that he was watching my every step. Not until I turned to walk straight at him did he flare up, but silently, as if he were too scared to cackle.

Later that same season it was my rare good fortune to see another cock pheasant use his wit when threatened by an enemy from whom he could not escape by running or flying or hiding. The occasion was a hunt for flight woodcock in a field of goldenrod that was going riotously to seed, filling the air with pollen dust which in a minute would spoil a dog's nose for the next hour. I was going around the field, my setter at heel, when I stopped to watch a goshawk that was acting erratically—swooping to the goldenrod tops, rising, swooping again. His every swoop was the signal for a violent motion below; some living thing was forcing a way through the weed stems.

When the chase passed out of sight behind a fringe of gray birches I ran around the field to find the hawk hovering over a tangle of dead weeds and blackberry briers beside a stone wall. Projecting out of the tangle was the tail of a cock pheasant that had forced his body under the briers where the hawk could not strike with his talons. Standing unnoticed under the birches, I watched for perhaps ten minutes. During that time

the hawk swooped again and again, only to rise when his sharp
claws gripped nothing but sharp briers. The cock never moved
a muscle, not even when the gun spoke and the killer thudded
down beside him. When booted out of the tangle he took to
wing, losing only a few feathers, and slanted up to a bower of
golden-tinted leaves in the top of a poplar. There he could not
be seen so long as he held still, and there we left him. Who
could shoot a bird after he had played a desperate life-or-death
game on sheer nerve—and won!

In a wild state pheasants feed twice daily, spending the midday hours loafing or dusting or otherwise enjoying life. Their
feeding place is wherever they find food they like—grain or
grasshoppers or ripe grapes or skunk-cabbage seeds—and it varies with the season. Their loafing place may be a cat-brier
thicket, a bog, a waste of weeds or scratchy raspberry vines—
in short, the meanest kind of cover. More interesting to one
who would learn how to hunt pheasants is the fact that, in
going from one feeding or loafing ground to another, they follow regular runways when they feel at ease, or regular flyways
if compelled to use their wings.

This runway habit was made plain to me by pheasants that
came daily to my feeding table. They always slipped over the
wall at the same spot, a gap left by a fallen stone; and I emphasize the "slipped" because they were so swift and secretive
about it. One might catch a fleeting glimpse as they dropped
from the gap into the shrubbery, not to be seen again until
they appeared at the table, which was purposely placed in the
open. Before coming over the wall they had followed the runway some two hundred yards, keeping all the while hidden
under low-branched evergreens. After feeding they would re-

cross the wall by the same gap and follow the runway back to their loafing ground.

On the other side of the wall was an open field, and across it was a runway used by a few pheasants from a distant estate. In autumn, when the field was bare, they would streak over this runway as if afraid of being seen; in summer they moved leisurely, their going traced by a wiggling of grass tops. It was here that an uncommonly large cock showed me that, wherever a runway has been established, every pheasant seems bound to follow it.

One morning I chanced to notice this old soldier limping up and down beside a woven-wire fence, about four feet high, which my neighbor had erected to keep a pet dog within bounds. A half hour later, when I went out to give my young setter Hiyu his morning brush-down, the cock was still limping up and down on his sentry-go, as if determined to find his lost runway or to force it open. With a hand wave in his direction I said, "Over you go, pup. Tell that cock pheasant what wings are for."

At the word Hiyu was over the wall. His eye caught the moving bird, but no scent came to his nose because of the wind; so he began a catlike sneak, slipping ahead when the cock moved away, stopping when the cock turned back, until he caught the body scent and froze in a beautiful point. The cock came limping back, frequently poking his head through the wire mesh in search of the lost runway until, suddenly, there in front of him was his dog enemy.

We are told that wild creatures follow one impulse at a time, or the stronger of two impulses, and this pheasant proved it. Up he towered heavily, almost straight up, in a belated impulse to escape. Hiyu cleared the fence as if pulled by the cock's tail, so close was his nose to it. At my sharp whistle he came running back, his plume merry, in his eye the plea of a happy child: "What fun! Let's do it again."

The lesson of the runway habit, I think, is this: When a pheasant takes to his legs he probably knows where he is going, and he will certainly stop when he gets there. He may run fifty yards or the better part of a mile if not pressed too hard; but, whenever he decides to rest in a safe hide-out, there he will stay until you all but step on him.

In that same Connecticut township I learned also that this exasperating foreigner can be driven to the gun like grouse, not by a noisy line of beaters, but by one man with a dog under control. The best of several covers was an open ridge which from a distance looked smoothly rounded but which was actually a series of low hills and hollows, many so well watered that hundreds of acres were formerly under cultivation.

At the foot of the western slope of this ridge was a narrow marsh, nearly a mile long from south to north, with bogs, alder thickets, and sunny openings carpeted by knee-high grass. One October morning when I was out for woodcock, my setter Rab took a hot trail into the lower end of the swamp, and I followed him with frequent checks until a cock pheasant cackled out of the extreme upper end. He was far out of range, but my eye followed his flight northeastward over an open slope, past a dead hickory to the top of a hill, where he set his wings and glided down to an unseen landing. Here was one flyway to be remembered. To find out where it ended I followed over the hill into a hollow, where Rab pointed in a thicket overrun by wild grapevines. The cock was in there, probably too leg-weary for another run; anyway, he flushed and came home in my shooting-coat pocket.

My next outing, which was not so much to hunt pheasants as to learn more of their natural ways, took me straight to the lower end of the same marsh. Within a few minutes Rab was trailing, and this time he was permitted to take his own gait, which was a deal faster than mine. He was about midway in the swamp when a cock pheasant cackled up from an opening and sped away eastward on a different flyway. Again we followed his flight, found where he hit the ground, and trailed him to an amazing hide-out. This was a natural hollow, about a dozen yards in diameter and I knew not how deep, heaped high with weathered boulders, which farmers of another generation had hauled out of their grain field and dumped here to be rid of them.

When a cock pheasant or any other game outwits me like that, I feel more inclined to doff my hat than to shoot him, but just for the fun of it I ordered Rab to seek. Around and over the bowl he went, poking his nose into one inviting hole after another. When his tail told me, "Here he is," I poked a stick into the hole. Once a faint, fluttery rumble told that the cock had moved, and presently Rab's tail was telling of another find. Wondering how long the cock would hold still, I went to smoke a pipe and enjoy the hilltop view for a full hour. Then we went silently around the bowl, but found no outgoing trail. The cock was safe in a refuge from which no dog could make him run or fly.

On a third outing that season I waved my setter into the lower end of the marsh, while I ran along the edge to take my stand in the midway opening. In a few minutes Rab appeared, moving fast where the scent was hot, or slowly where the cock stirred up an unclean smell by running through stagnant water. Saw grass wiggled ahead of him, coming nearer, and I stepped in front of it to scare the running bird into the air. But again I was outwitted. Around my feet he streaked, a flash of living color under the dead grass. Then came Rab, so intent on the reek in his nose that he paid me no attention, not even a look, when he whipped past under the gun muzzle. A minute or two later a cock flushed from the upper end of the marsh to follow precisely the same course, past the dead hickory and over the hill.

These two flyways—one from the upper end of the marsh to the grapevines, the other from the midway opening to the rock bowl—were used by every cock pheasant in the locality, and the lonely marsh was a favorite hangout.

One day when my setter found a cock in the upper end of the marsh, the cock went out of cover on his legs, heading over the hill toward the grapevines. It took me some twenty minutes to move around the hill in order to approach the grapevines from the farther side; and all that time the cock was resting after his run. This time he went out of the grapevines on his legs, not on his wings. As my setter trailed him along the ridge side a fascinating story came to light. Straight past the waiting gun he streaked, hidden by some weeds, and turned up the ridge to find refuge in the rock bowl.

From several such happy adventures come certain conclusions which I think are valid. Although a cock pheasant runs fast for a short distance, so fast that a man or a slow dog is outdistanced, a long run tires him and he must rest. By a long run I mean fifty or sixty yards if he is hard pushed, or a half mile if you let him stop occasionally by checking the dog. In either case he will probably make his next getaway on his wings. A long flight also tires him and if approached before his wings are rested he will almost certainly take to his legs. If a long run is followed by a long flight he will lie so close to a point that you must literally boot him out of hiding. Twice have I seen a spaniel and once an unsteady pointer jump on a cock pheasant before he could make up his mind whether to fly or run or to chance it by holding still.

Many sportsmen have denounced the pheasant as a nuisance, saying that he spoils their trained dogs by his habit of running away from a point. The natural answer is, first, that a pheasant depends on his long legs for travel, like a wild turkey, using his short wings only as a last resort; and, second, that whether dealing with men or other enemies it is safer to run away under cover than to flaunt his gaudy colors in the open. Almost invariably they run away from a point.

The whole "secret" of successful trailing, to my mind, is to take it easy, especially when the scent grows warm and both dog and man are naturally inclined to hurry. So long as a cock thinks he is winning the race he will make shorter runs and stops until he comes to the hide-out he has in mind, and then he will at last "hold" to a point. If pushed too hard he will naturally take to his faster wings and be out of range before you see or hear him.

In the matter of releasing farm-raised pheasants, which looks easy but is hard to do well, there are two lessons which I, working with my local sportsmen's club, learned by the trial-and-error method.

One year, with the shooting season only two weeks distant, we were notified to receive a shipment of a hundred pheasants, which must promptly be released in covers open to all licensed sportsmen. They came by truck on time, and such a scrawny lot of half-fledged chicks I had never imagined.

So instead of releasing them, we made arrangements to winter them at our own expense on a private estate which had two empty holding pens and a gamekeeper who knew his business. No word came from the commissioner when we notified him of the club's action, adding that his order to release such unfit birds would be obeyed under protest. In the spring, after a loss of only three, we released ninety-seven full-grown birds as breeding stock in our empty covers.

When farm-raised birds are released in selected cover there are usually too many helpers present; and however careful you may be, there is no way to predict how the bewildered birds will react when suddenly confronted with liberty for the first time in their lives. I have repeatedly seen some of them take to their wings and fly out of sight. Others have run so far, like a man lost in the woods, that a few days later my setter could find no trace of them.

So a new plan was tried one spring when the club bought two dozen hen pheasants and as many cocks as breeding stock. On a game farm five or six hens and one cock are confined in a small pen during the breeding season; no nests are built, and eggs are collected twice daily. In open covers, where pheasants naturally scatter and every hen steals away to hide her nest, the best results in the way of increase are obtained, I think, when the sexes are about equal in number.

The place selected for the "planting" was a valley, about five miles long, where formerly I had found both quail and ruffed grouse. It was now practically empty of game except for a few woodcock in the flight season. The cover varied from alder swamp to brushy hillside, from wood lots to abandoned farm lands that were growing up to weeds, and through the middle of it meandered a lazy little brook. Food, water, and shelter—here were the three prime requisites.

Before the breeding stock arrived I had built a temporary holding pen in a wood lot about in the middle of the valley. On the brook side of the pen the chicken wire ended about six inches above the ground, leaving a wide gate which was closed by a board standing on edge and held upright by stakes. From the gate three diverging runways were cleared of leaves and sprinkled with grain, which became more abundant with increasing distance from the pen. The psychological idea was to keep the birds wholly intent on food at first, and not on the new liberty to run or fly as they pleased.

At nightfall, when birds are naturally quiet, the pheasants were transferred one by one from the crates into the holding pen. A single helper was enough; all he had to do was to lie quietly on his stomach and open or close the gate at a nod. Before sunrise next morning, while the wood was in deep shadow, I crept to the pen alone and very slowly pulled the gate open, and crept away again. Not a pheasant moved or squawked; they did not even know that they were being set free. From a distance I watched them leave the pen to follow the prepared runways, feeding as they went, until they vanished by twos and threes into the waiting cover.

That was the only time when released pheasants with a lunatic streak in their make-up did as we had planned for them. On my return to the scene one cock was crowing loudly near at hand, another faintly in the distance. So does the ruffed grouse summon a mate by sending his drum call through the budding woods. A few weeks later I found a nest with fourteen eggs, so cunningly hidden that I almost stepped on it. In midsummer, on a still hunt which covered only a fraction of the valley, I found two broods, each of about eight or ten chicks, but they winked away from under my setter's nose before they could be counted. More broods were reported from other parts of the range, indicating that the breeding stock was well scattered. Then the little brook shrank to a trickle and we faced a new problem, which for the moment threatened plenty of trouble.

Unknown to the club members, an Italian gardener had leased four acres of good land in the valley, which by hard labor he had turned into an enormous tomato garden. It was within sight of where the pheasants were released, and by ill luck the brook had there run dry. Presently the Italian was bombarding the town fathers with complaints that some accursed big birds were eating his tomatoes before they got ripe. And if the fathers did not do something about it *subito*, he would do it himself with a shotgun.

Hearing of the complaint and feeling a bit guilty, I went first to gauge the damage for myself. Along one edge of the garden, facing the dried-up brook, every second or third big tomato had a neatly punctured hole at its top and on one side; when pressed by my fingers it collapsed, leaving only the tough skin and the unripe seeds. Pheasant tracks told all too plainly who had punctured the tomatoes. But they couldn't be hungry, not at this season with its abundant plant and animal food. Finding the brook dry, they had simply come to the tomato garden as to an unfailing soda fountain.

With this one fact for comfort I went to the Italian's house that same evening. The troublesome big birds were pheasants, he was told. They came to his garden, not for food, but because they were thirsty, poor things. Maybe if we put some crocks of water at the edge of his garden the pheasants would drink it instead of sucking his tomatoes. If he were willing to try the experiment, my club would furnish the water crocks and pay half the labor cost of keeping them filled.

It is a pleasure to record that the Italian was also a sportsman at heart. It was a pity, he said, that any creature should suffer from thirst. Yes, he would be glad to co-operate. So the water-crock experiment was tried and, believe it or not, it worked. There were no more complaints, and the gardener harvested a very good crop.

The shooting season brought a greater problem for which there was no answer. Whether because of good breeding stock, good cover, or good weather, or all three factors combined, that spring planting of mature pheasants was the most success-ful of the club's many efforts to provide more game birds. We raised a goodly number of wild pheasants, certainly, but there was no way to regulate either the number of hunters or the hours of hunting. Rumor spread through the county that pheasants were plentiful in a certain locality, and on opening day the whole valley was swept from end to end by a score or more hunters with their dogs. There was hardly a day when every good cover was not harried at least once.

The inevitable result was that some pheasants were quickly "shot out" and all the rest driven out. No game will stay where its feeding and resting hours are constantly disturbed. So our club faced the question of whether to put our money into breeding stock again, or save time and work by buying farm-raised pheasants that would quickly be shot.

For me there is only one answer. It is no pleasure for me to shoot a farm-raised bird of any kind. Aside from that, a pheasant raised in the wild learns from infancy how to take care of himself, as farm-raised birds cannot possibly learn. By the time he is grown to shootable size he knows every feeding place, loafing place, and hiding place on his wide range. From constant exercise he runs faster than the farm-raised bird; he flies more speedily and to a greater distance; he is much harder to find. At times he gives the impression that, like a crow, he learns to let you come *almost* within shooting distance before he is off with a *kak-kak-kak* of derision.

In other words, the wild-raised pheasant is in every way a more sporty bird because, being a part of wild nature from birth, he calls for more skill, more wit, and far more leg work on the hunter's part. He is game for the sportsman who goes afield for the pleasure of hunting, first of all, and comes home at twilight glad at heart, whether his gamebag is full or empty.

Crow Talk

THE time is late afternoon of an August day; the place, a salmon-fishing camp on the Tobique. Shadows are rising like a flood tide on eastern hills; the west is aglow with sunset splendor. We sit on the porch of my cabin; our bodies are at rest, minds open, senses attuned to a harmony like the peace of God that comes at evening to the wilderness.

On the topmost twig of a towering larch a male robin sings his vesper song; by the ruddy reflection on his breast you may know that he still sees a light which has dropped below our forest-fringed horizon. From his muted Angelus our attention is rudely drawn to the unmelodious talking of crows on a wooded ridge beyond the singing river.

The word "talk" is used here deliberately, not to suggest that crows have a language, but to emphasize the fact that the sound they make as dusky-winged twilight glides over the land-scape is very different from the daylight clamor, raucous and senseless, when crows have cornered an enemy—hawk or owl or fox or bobcat—and are telling the world what a villain he is and what they would do to him if they could. They are then very much like an excited human mob, mindless and mannerless, when fear or hate or some other poisonous passion is in the saddle.

Even in such moments of emotional madness, when crows respond instinctively to the ancient rally cry of the flock, they always leave a door open for the entrance of method. As an illuminating example, once while I was roaming the woods an uproar to westward told me that crows might be chivvying a young eagle I had been observing in hope of learning how he fared in foraging for himself. Stealing from cover to cover, I had drawn near the clamor when one careless step cracked a twig, a feeble alarm but enough to cause an instant motion of wings overhead. From his hide-out in the top of a spruce a crow shot away toward the frenzied flock, crying his alarm note. From the heart of a scrub pine a large hawk slipped away in the opposite direction, and from the top of another evergreen a second crow followed the hawk silently.

Evidently, two crows were keeping watch over a hawk while many others dealt with the hawk's mate—or so it seemed to me at the time and place. As quietly as possible I hurried toward the clamoring flock, but I was too late. The sentinel was ahead of me. At his warning the crows all whirled away northward; how they had detected his voice in a din that deafened my ears only a crow might tell. A flicker of wings was all that could be seen of the hawk they were baiting. As she sped away westward to safety, there came from far to eastward a high-pitched signal, as if the second sentinel were telling of the other hawk, "Here he is! I see the rascal!" That the crows understood him could hardly be doubted by one who saw them turn swiftly in his direction. And presently in good hiding I was enjoying another hawk baiting, from which the victim escaped at last by mounting in a spiral to a height so dizzy that the crows dared not follow. By twos and threes they abandoned the chase and dropped to safety in the treetops.

All this excitement of an earlier day is forgotten as we sit on the porch of my cabin, harking to a flock of crows and hearing talk that, by comparison, is quietly rational rather than noisily emotional. For fifty years and more, morning or midday or evening, I have heard such talk with its short or long calls, its evenly spaced pauses; but only recently has it occurred to me that one might learn to interpret or understand it by observing how the crows react to every call.

Before venturing on this unblazed trail, let me explain that these crows are in many ways different from the sable bandits of pasture and farm land. Here in the wilderness where their increase is kept in check by natural enemies, they are much less numerous than in long-settled regions and in consequence less destructive to other birds. They are also more shy, more solitary, and much more suspicious of humanity for the evident reason that they have no knowledge gained by experience of man or his ways or his limitations.

Around farm land, for example, you can get almost but not quite within shooting distance of an observant crow; he seems to know when you are near enough to be dangerous. The wilderness crow is off while you are yet at a distance, and you will not get even a glimpse of him if he sees you first. In the woods near my home I can call crows over me at almost any hour or season. Even after some of their number have been shot as

nest robbers, the flock can be recalled by changing the summons to the distress call of a young crow or to the owl-baiting
yell of a veteran. But somehow these wilderness crows have my
number, or whatever it is that rings a bell when they hear
me. Many have answered my call at a distance; never have I
been able to lure one over my hiding place.

This excessive wariness is, I think, a result of their environment and early training. Each crow family seems to have a few
square miles of its own territory, larger or smaller according to
food or forage conditions, just as a pair of loons or sheldrakes
or kingfishers have each a different portion of a lake or river.
Since in the northern woods there is only one mated pair of
crows within a radius of two or three miles, the probable reason
why they do not come to my call is that, being familiar with
every voice on their range, they easily recognize mine as a fraud.
In the neighborhood of our towns, by contrast, there are too
many voices, calls, noises, and other disturbances of the peace
for any crow or man to place them.

As the summer wanes, young crows who have been reared
in solitude gather with other family groups in obedience to
their social instinct. In this respect they are like the dusky mal-
lards or the caribou that once abounded in this Tobique country. Often of an afternoon, when the crows are well fed and
therefore playful, they may be seen practicing a kind of wing
drill of which the young are playfully ignorant but as the old
know by experience is a preparation for the massed autumn
flight to the seacoast. When winter comes to the wilderness
there will be no crows to talk or clamor here. Only their big
relative, Kakagos, the raven, will float like a dark shadow over
a solitude that appears to be lifeless, its white face upturned
to the cold gray sky.

Long before the autumn migration, all crow families for ten or twenty miles around gather nightly at a common roosting place which must be carefully chosen and guarded because this is the time and place of greatest danger. Farmland or sea-coast crows have the same habit, and you may have noticed how cautious is their approach to the roost. They light at a distance, invariably on open ground where no bushes interfere with their vision; they powwow for a time, with a deal of chatter; they send a few scouts ahead, as if to be sure that the roost hides no human enemy; and at last by small companies they slip in from the downwind side, silent as so many shadows.

In the wilderness, crows are even more cautious because their natural enemies are more numerous, more expert, and much less easily detected. Kupkawis, the barred owl, and Kookooskoos, the horned owl, hunt by night on wings that make no sound. That they snatch many a sleeping crow from the roost is about the only good thing you can say of big owls, of Kookooskoos especially. They are relentless killers of small game, to be sure; yet they kill many crows also, and every surviving crow nourishes its brood on the eggs and nestlings of quail, grouse, ducks, and a multitude of song and insectivorous birds.

On a wooded ridge across the river from my cabin is a roost, so near that you can hear and even distinguish the different crow voices. A short time ago there were four family groups, or about a dozen birds all told; now the number has more than doubled. The voices of the parent birds are deeper, stronger, more authoritative. Young voices are at first all alike to human ears. But in a little while you may learn to recognize one crow that sounds a contented note; another is complaining, as if hungry; a third is inquisitive or lazy or domineering—precisely the same tonal differences that you hear in the voices of children at play in the schoolyard.

The assembled crows are not yet in their roost, which is under the crest of the ridge; they are drawing near to it slowly, in that habitually careful way which speaks of both instinct and intelligence. A little while ago they were powwowing in an abandoned clearing, a half mile behind our camp; now they are scattered in a semicircle of dense woods, and they are not only talking but speaking in turn.

On the right of the semicircle, nearest the river, the voice of an old crow calls, *ka-ka, ka, ka,* four short notes, quiet but alert, with a very short interval between the first two and a longer interval before the third and fourth. Although by habit one writes *caw* or *haw,* the sound is purely vowel, sometimes like *a* as in "far," or again like *au* as in "maul." Around the whole wide semicircle goes the watchful signal, the same four notes on the same medium pitch with the same short and long pauses. There is an interval of silence, lasting about a half minute by my watch; then the same call goes the round once more from right to left.

Many times I have heard that signal when the crows were drawing near their roost, and only on rare occasions has it varied. Once, when the silent interval had lasted only a few seconds, a crow from the center of the semicircle started the call over again. To judge by his voice alone, he was an impatient young crow. That he spoke out of order was my inference from the blank silence which followed this break in the routine. I myself was feeling impatient at the long-continued pause, asking what it meant, when the youngster snapped out the regular call, to which he added a fifth and more peremptory note, as if he were demanding, "Why don't you answer me?" From the far left end of the semicircle a deep old voice spoke sharply, just once. Then the same quiet signal went the round once more, as if every crow was standing guard over his own portion of woods and reporting in turn, "All's well here."

This may or may not have been what the crows were saying or thinking; but it is a matter of record that the same call is heard every evening and is repeated at regular intervals for a quarter hour or less. After that the last notes of the signal are omitted, and for a shorter time a quieter *ka-ka* goes round the semicircle.

Twilight has begun to shadow the wooded steep when a deep and, as it seems to me, a solemn voice calls, *ka*, a single note, and all the crows are silent. Not another voice is heard or will be heard until after daybreak. Twice have I listened until past midnight. Once I climbed the pitch-dark ridge; but if owls raided the roost, as probably they did, the crows made no outcry. Many other birds give voice in the night, and some birds sing. Although I have elsewhere purposely disturbed a roost after the crows had gone to rest, never have I heard any talk or clamor from them, but only a flapping of wings or a scraping of twigs as some young crow blundered to another perch in the darkness.

Is this night silence of the crow merely a fixed habit, I wonder, or does it mean that he uses his head at a time when only stillness may save him from owlish eyes and ears that catch every slightest sound or motion. Some people cry out when frightened in the dark; others take the more intelligent and, usually, the safer course by remaining quiet.

There were different calls, all subdued by contrast with day voices, as the crows gathered to their roosting place; but this "All's well," if such were its import, stood out above all others, being repeated most often, most regularly, and, as I thought with a new wonder, most in accord with our age-old habit of passing the word from sentinel to sentinel. So the young crows were being trained, subconsciously it may be, for a time soon to come when they must take their place amid hundreds of strange crows that gather nightly from widely scattered feeding grounds to the common roost.

The morning talk of these wilderness crows was quite different, more eager and unrestrained, and much more difficult to interpret. At daybreak the robin that had put the sun to bed would from lofty treetop call the sun up again. As he is the last to chant "Good night," so the robin is always first to carol "Good morning." A little later, while the roost was still in shadow, I would hear a single call, loud and resonant, and then a chattered medley of which one could make no head or tail. It ceased for a few hours, leaving the woods all still while crow families scattered to their several forage grounds, but was renewed with gusto at midday, thus reminding me of what seems to be a universal corvine habit.

A pair of mated crows, as you may have noted, are very quiet when nesting and rearing their young, speaking softly to one another, telling nothing to the world. They are silent also when feeding, and when on the hunt for a brood of young ducks or partridges they are as stealthy as a stalking cat. They become talkative only on social occasions, or vociferous when they rally to a cry of alarm or distress.

Late summer and early fall are for the crows, as for most other birds, a time for play, for merrymaking, and therefore for much talk. The old have left nesting cares behind them; the young are strong of wing, and food with its corollary of natural content is everywhere abundant. So it happened one August afternoon, when crow voices were jubilant in the lonely and lovely Tobique Valley, that it came to my mind to make a firsthand study of crow talk as a new subject.

It was like an invitation, so pleasantly surprising that one wondered why no naturalist had ever before accepted it. At every idle hour after midday I followed the reassembled flock, harking to the different voices, memorizing each distinct call, and trying to match it with resultant crow action. For by his action alone can we interpret the mentality of any wild creature. To pry into the mood behind his action is to deal with a mystery, ignorantly. As Vergil said to Dante on their journey through Inferno, "What caution men must use who look not at the deed itself but spy into the thought!"

Very soon it became apparent that a high-pitched call meant one thing to the crows, and a similar call on a low pitch meant a different thing: to one they gathered quickly, to the other they remained indifferent. The chief difficulty in interpreting their many calls, aside from the gulf which separates man from the lower orders, was that too often they detected my approach and went on swift wings where human feet could not follow.

One fascinating and possibly a more significant thing about my Tobique crows was that their talk frequently took dialogue form. I listened from a hidden stand on the edge of a clearing where a few crows (but never the whole flock) often gathered to feed.

From his grasshopper or grub hunting a crow flew up to a treetop and sent forth a call of two or more notes, uttered at evenly spaced intervals; after which he assumed a tense or listening attitude, as I could plainly see. Far back in the forest or from the edge of a distant clearing another crow repeated the message precisely: the same notes, the same pitch, the same long or short intervals, and then an added note or two as of comment or objection. Whereupon the first crow either sent back the original message unchanged, or else repeated the new version as if in agreement.

To hear such a dialogue twice might be a mere coincidence. To hear it several times every afternoon, day after day, is to put chance out of the question and to suggest by analogy something remotely akin to the dots and dashes of the Morse alphabet—a talk which to untrained ears is but a meaningless series of clicks and silences.

Crows are intelligent birds, at times so surprising in their intelligence that one remembers with regret that they are nest robbers. When my Tobique summer went to join all other summers and vacation days came to an end too soon, my lasting impression was that crows understand their own talk perfectly. Some day, it may be, a lucky naturalist will find the key to it.

Cloud-Wings, the Eagle

"*HERE* he is again! Here's Old Whitehead, robbing the fish hawk."

I started up from the little *commoosie* beyond the fire, at my friend's excited cry, and ran to join him on the shore. I looked out over Caribou Point to the big bay, where innumerable whitefish were shoaling. Ismaquehs, the fish hawk, had risen from the lake with a big fish and was doing his best to get away with it to his nest, where his young ones were clamoring. Over him soared the eagle, as still and as sure as fate, now dropping to flap a wing in Ismaquehs' face, now touching him gently with his great talons, as if to say, "Do you feel that, Ismaquehs? If I grip once it will be the end of you and your fish together. Better drop him peacefully."

Up to that moment the eagle had merely bothered the big

hawk's flight, with a gentle reminder now and then that he meant no harm but wanted the fish which he could not catch himself. Now there was a change, a flash of the king's temper. With a roar of wings he whirled about the hawk like a tempest, bringing up short and fierce, squarely in his line of flight. There he poised on dark broad wings, his yellow eyes glaring fiercely into the shrinking soul of Ismaquehs, his talons drawn back for a deadly strike. And Simmo the Indian, who had run down to join me, muttered: "Cheplahgan mad now. Ismaquehs find-um out in a minute."

But Ismaquehs knew just when to stop. With a cry of rage he dropped, or rather threw, his fish, hoping it would strike the water and be lost. Immediately the eagle wheeled out of the way and bent his head sharply. I had seen him fold his wings and drop before and I had held my breath at the speed, but dropping was of no use now, for the fish fell faster. Instead he swooped downward, adding the push of his strong wings to the weight of his fall, glancing down like a bolt to catch the fish before it struck the water, and rising again in a great curve—up and away steadily, evenly, as the king should fly, to his own little ones far away on the mountain.

Weeks before, on the Madawaska, I had had my introduction to Old Whitehead. Gillie and I were pushing up the river on our way to the wilderness, when a great outcry and the noise of a gun sounded just ahead. Dashing around a wooded bend, we came upon a man with a smoking gun, a boy up to his middle in the river, trying to get across, and, on the other side, a black sheep running about baaing at every jump.

"He's taken the lamb; he's taken the lamb!" shouted the boy. Following the direction of his pointing finger, I saw Old Whitehead, a splendid bird, rising heavily above the treetops across the clearing. Reaching back almost instinctively, I clutched the heavy rifle which Gillie put into my hand and jumped out of the canoe. It was a long shot, but not so very difficult. Old Whitehead had his bearings and was moving steadily, straight away. A second after the report of the rifle, we saw him hitch and swerve in the air; then two white quills came floating down, and as he turned we saw the break in his broad white tail. And that was the mark that we knew him by ever afterwards.

From where we now stood that was nearly eighty miles by canoe, although scarcely ten in a straight line over the mountains; for the rivers and lakes we were following doubled back almost to the starting point; and the whole wild, splendid country was the eagle's hunting ground. Wherever I went I saw him, following the rivers for stranded trout and salmon or floating high in the air where he could overlook two or three wilderness lakes, where honest fish hawks were catching their dinners. I had promised the curator of a museum that I would get him an eagle that summer, and so I took to hunting the great bird diligently. But hunting was of little use, except to teach me many of his ways and habits. He seemed to have eyes and ears all over him; and whether I crept like a snake through the woods or floated like a wild duck in my canoe over the water, he always saw or heard me and was off before I could get within shooting distance.

Then I tried to trap him. I placed two large trout, with a steel trap between them, at a shallow spot in the river that I could watch from my camp bluff, half a mile below. Next day Gillie, who was more eager than I, set up a shout; and running out, I saw Old Whitehead standing in the shallows and flopping about the trap. We jumped into a canoe and pushed upriver in hot haste, exulting that we had the fierce old bird at last. When we had doubled the last point that hid the shallows, there was Old Whitehead, still tugging away at a fish and splashing the water not thirty yards away. I shall never forget his attitude and expression as we shot around the point. His body was erect and rigid, his wings half spread, his head thrust forward, eyelids drawn straight, and there was a strong fierce gleam of freedom and utter wildness in his bright eyes. So he stood, a magnificent creature, until we were almost upon him—when he rose quietly, taking one of the trout. The other was already in his stomach. He was not in the trap at all, but had walked around it carefully. The splashing was made as he tore one fish to pieces with his claws and as he freed the other from the stake that held it.

After that he would not go near the shallows, for a new experience had come into his life, leaving its shadow dark behind it. He who was king of all he surveyed from the old blasted pine on the crag's top, who had always heretofore been the hunter, now knew what it meant to be hunted. And the fear of it was in his eyes, I think; it softened their fierce gleam when I looked into them again, weeks later, by his own nest on the mountain.

Simmo entered into our hunting also, but without enthusiasm or confidence. He had chased the same eagle before—all one summer, in fact, when a sportsman whom he was guiding had offered him twenty dollars for the royal bird's skin. But Old Whitehead still wore it triumphantly, and Simmo prophesied for him long life and a natural death. "No use hunt-um dat eagle," he said simply. "He sees everyt'ing; and wot he don't see, he hear. 'Sides, he kin *feel* danger. Das why he build nest way off, long ways—oh, don' know where." Cheplahgan, Old Cloud-Wings, he called the bird that had defied him in a summer's hunting.

At first I had hunted him like any other wild thing—partly, of course, to get his skin for the curator; partly, perhaps, to save the settler's lambs over on the Madawaska; but chiefly just to kill him, to exult in his death flaps, and to rid the woods of a cruel tyrant. Gradually, however, a change came over me as I hunted; I sought him less and less for his skin and his life, and more and more for myself, to know all about him. I used to watch him by the hour from my camp on the big lake, sailing quietly over Caribou Point, after he had eaten with his little ones and was disposed to let Ismaquehs go on with his fishing in peace. He would set his great wings to the breeze and sit like a kite in the wind, mounting steadily in an immense spiral, up and up, without a shadow of effort, until the eye grew dizzy in following. And I loved to watch him, so strong, so free, so sure of himself—round and round, up and ever up, without hurry, without exertion—as at every turn he found the heavens nearer and the earth spread wider below. His head and tail gleamed silver white in the sunshine; then he would hang motionless against the clear, unfathomable blue of the June heavens; then he was lost in the blue, so high that I could not see any more. But even as I turned away he would plunge down into vision again, dropping with folded wings straight down like a plummet, faster and faster, larger and larger, through a terrifying rush of air, until I sprang to my feet and caught my breath, as if I myself were falling. And just before it seemed he would dash himself to pieces he turned in the air, head downward, and half spread his wings and went shooting, slanting down toward the lake, then up in a great curve to the treetops, where he could watch better what Kakagos, the rare woods raven, was doing and what game he was hunting. For that was what Cheplaghan came down in such a hurry to find out about.

Again he would come in the early morning, sweeping up the river as if he had already been on a long day's journey, with the air of faraway and far-to-go in his onward rush. And if I were at the trout pools and very still, I would hear the strong silken rustle of his wings as he passed. At midday I would see him poised over the highest mountaintop northward, at an enormous altitude, where imagination itself could not follow the splendid sweep of his vision; and at evening he would cross the lake, moving westward into the sunset on tireless pinions—always strong, noble, magnificent in his power and loneliness, a perfect emblem of the great, lonely, magnificent wilderness.

One day as I watched him, it swept over me suddenly that forest and river would be incomplete without him. The thought of this came back to me, and spared him to the wilderness, on the last occasion when I went hunting for his life.

That was just after we reached the big lake, where I saw him robbing the fish hawk. After much searching and watching I found a great log by the outlet, where Old Whitehead often perched. There was a big eddy nearby on the edge of a shallow, and he used to sit on the log, waiting for fish to come out to where he could wade in and get them. There was a sickness among the suckers that year and they would come struggling out of deep water to rest on the sand, only to be caught by the minks and fish hawks and bears and Old Whitehead, all of whom were waiting and hungry for fish.

For several days I put a big bait of trout and whitefish on the edge of the shallows. The first two baits were put out late in the afternoon, and a bear got them both that night. Then I put them out in the early morning, and before noon Cheplahgan had found them. He came straight over from his watch place

on the mountains, miles away, causing me to wonder greatly
what strange sixth sense guided him, for sight and smell seemed
equally out of the question. The next day he came again. Then
I placed the best bait of all in the shallows, and hid in the dense
underbrush near, with my gun.

After hours of waiting, he came at last, dropping from above
the treetops with a heavy rustling of pinions. As he touched the
old log and spread his broad white tail, I saw and was proud
of the gap which my bullet had made weeks before. He stood
there a moment, erect and splendid, head, neck, and tail shining
white; even the dark brown feathers of his body glinted in the
bright sunshine. And he turned his head slowly from side to
side, his keen eyes flashing, as if he would say, "Behold, a king!"
Then he hopped down—rather awkwardly, it must be con-
fessed; for he is a creature who cannot bear to touch the ground
—seized a fish, which he tore to pieces with his claws and ate
greedily. Twice I tried to shoot him; but the thought of the
wilderness without him was upon me and held me back. Then,
too, it seemed mean to fire at him from ambush when he had
come down to earth, where he was at a disadvantage; and when
he clutched some of the larger fish in his talons and rose swiftly
and bore away westward, all desire to kill him was gone. There
were little Cloud-Wings, which I must also find and watch.
After that I hunted him more diligently than before, but without my gun. And a curious desire, which I could not account
for, took possession of me: to touch this untamed, untouched
creature of the clouds and mountains.

Next day I did it. There was a thick bush growing along one
end of the old log on which the eagle rested. Into this I cut a
tunnel with my hunting knife, arranging the top in such a way

as to screen me more effectively. Then I put out my bait, a good two hours before the time of Old Whitehead's earliest appearance, and crawled into my den to wait.

I had barely settled comfortably into my place when a heavy silken rustle sounded close at hand, and I heard the grip of his talons on the log. There he stood, an arm's length from me, turning his head uneasily, the light glinting on his white crest, the fierce, untamed flash in his bright eye. Never before had he seemed so big, so strong, so splendid.

But I had little time to think, for Cheplahgan was restless. Some instinct seemed to warn him of a danger that he could not see. The moment his head was turned away, I stretched out my arm. Scarcely a leaf moved with the motion, yet he whirled like a flash and crouched to spring, his eyes glaring straight into mine with an intensity that I could scarcely endure. Perhaps I was mistaken, but in that swift instant the hard glare in his eyes seemed to soften with fear, as he recognized me as the one thing in the wilderness that dared to hunt him, the king. My hand touched him fair on the shoulder; then he shot into the air and went sweeping in great circles over the treetops, still looking down at the man, wondering and fearing at the way in which he had been brought into the man's power.

But one thing he did not understand. Standing erect on the log and looking up at him as he swept over me, I kept thinking, "I did it, I did it, Cheplahgan, Old Cloud-Wings. And I chose to let you go free."

For several days I had been watching Old Whitehead's lines of flight, and I had concluded that his nest was somewhere in the hills northwest of the big lake. I went there one afternoon, and I saw, not Old Whitehead, but a larger eagle, his mate undoubtedly, flying with food straight westward toward a great cliff that I had noticed with my glass one day from a mountain on the other side of the lake.

When I went there, early next morning, it was Cheplahgan himself who showed me where his nest was. I was hunting along the foot of the cliff when, glancing back toward the lake, I saw him coming far away, and I hid in the underbrush. He passed very near, and, following, I saw him standing on a ledge near the top of the cliff. Just below him, in the top of a stunted tree growing out of the face of the rock, was a huge mass of sticks that formed the nest; a great mother eagle stood by, feeding the little ones. Both birds started away silently when I appeared, but they came back soon and swept back and forth over me as I sat watching the nest and the face of the cliff through my glass. There was now no need for caution. Both birds seemed to know instinctively why I had come, and that the fate of the eaglets lay in my hands, if I could scale the cliff.

It was scary business, that three-hundred-foot climb up the sheer face of the mountain. Fortunately the rock was seamed and scarred with the wear of the centuries; bushes and stunted trees grew out of countless crevices, which gave me sure footing and sometimes a lift of a dozen feet or more on my way up. As I climbed, the eagles circled lower and lower; the strong rustling of their wings was about my head continually; they seemed to grow larger, fiercer every moment, as my hold grew more precarious and the earth below and the pointed treetops dropped further away.

There was a good revolver in my pocket, to use in case of necessity; but had the great birds attacked me I should have fared badly; for at times I was obliged to grip hard with both hands, my face to the cliff, leaving the eagles free to strike from above and behind. I think now that had I shown fear in such a place, or shouted, or tried to drive them away, they would have swooped down upon me, wing and claw, like furies. I could see it in their fierce eyes as I looked up. But the thought of the times when I had hunted him, especially the thought of that time when I reached out of the bush and touched him, was upon Old Whitehead and made him fear. So I kept steadily on my way, apparently giving no thought to the eagles, although deep inside I was anxious enough, and I reached the foot of the tree in which the nest was made.

With my arm clasping the twisted old bole, I stood there a long time, looking out over the forest spread wide below, partly to regain my courage, partly to reassure the eagles, which were circling very near with a kind of intense wonder in their eyes, but mostly to make up my mind about what to do next. The tree was easy to climb, but the nest—a huge affair which had been added to year after year—filled the whole treetop, and I could gain no foothold from which to look over and see the eaglets without tearing the nest to pieces. I did not want to do that; and I doubted whether the mother eagle would stand for it. A dozen times she seemed on the point of dropping on my head to tear it with her talons; but always she veered off as I looked up quietly, and Old Whitehead, with the mark of my bullet strong upon him, swept between her and me and seemed to say, "Wait, wait! I don't understand; but he can kill us if he will—and the little ones are in his power." Now he was closer to me than ever, and the fear was vanishing. And so was the fierceness.

From the foot of the tree the crevice in which it grew led to the right, then doubled back above the nest to the ledge upon which Cheplahgan was standing when I discovered him. The lip of this crevice made a dizzy path that I could follow by moving crabwise, my face to the cliff, with only its roughness to cling to with my fingers. I tried it at last; crept up and out twenty feet, and back ten, and dropped with a great breath of relief to a broad ledge covered with bones and fish scales, the relics of many a wild feast. Below me, almost within reach, was the nest, with two dark, scraggly young birds resting on twigs and grass, with fish, flesh, and fowl in a gory, skinny, scaly ring about them—the most savage-looking household I had ever seen.

But even as I looked a strange thing happened, which touched me as few things ever have among the wild creatures. The eagles had followed me close along the last edge of rock, hoping, no doubt, in their wild hearts that I would slip, and end their troubles, and give my body as food to the young. Now, as I sat on the ledge, peering eagerly into the nest, the great mother bird left me and hovered over her eaglets, as if to shield them with her wings from even the sight of my eyes. But Old Whitehead still circled over me. He came lower and lower, until with a supreme effort of daring he folded his wings and dropped to the ledge beside me, within ten feet, where he turned and looked into my eyes. "See," he seemed to say, "we are within reach again. You touched me once; I don't know how or why. Here I am now, to touch or to kill, as you will; only spare the little ones."

A moment later the mother bird dropped to the edge of the nest. And there we sat, we three, with the wonder upon us all, the young eagles at our feet, and the cliff above, and, three hundred feet below, the spruce tops of the wilderness reaching out and away to the mountains beyond the big lake.

I sat perfectly still, and soon I thought Cheplahgan had lost his fear in his anxiety for the little ones. But the moment I rose to go he was in the air again, circling restlessly above my head with his mate, the same wild fierceness in his eyes as he looked down. A half hour later I had gained the top of the cliff and started eastward toward the lake, coming down by a much easier way than that by which I went up. Later I returned several times and from a distance watched the eaglets being fed. But I never climbed to the nest again.

One day, when I came to the little thicket on the cliff where I used to lie and watch the nest through my glass, I found that one eaglet was gone. The other stood on the edge of the nest, looking down fearfully into the abyss and calling disconsolately from time to time. His whole attitude showed plainly that he was hungry and cross and lonesome. Presently the mother eagle came swiftly up from the valley, and there was food in her talons. She came to the edge of the nest, hovered over it a moment to give the hungry eaglet a sight and smell of the food, then went slowly down to the valley, taking the food with her, telling the little one in her own way to come and he should have it. From the edge of the nest he called after her loudly and spread his wings a dozen times to follow. But the plunge was too awful; his heart failed him; and he settled back in the nest, pulled his head down into his shoulders, shut his eyes, and tried to forget that he was hungry. The meaningful little comedy was plain enough. She was trying to teach him to fly, telling him that his wings were grown and the time was come to use them; but he was afraid.

In a little while she came back again, this time without food, and hovered over the nest, trying every way to induce the little one to leave it. She succeeded at last, when with a desperate effort he sprang upward and flapped to the ledge above where I had sat and watched him with Old Whitehead. Then, after surveying the world gravely from his new place, he flapped back to the nest and turned a deaf ear to all his mother's assurances that he could fly just as easily to the treetops below, if he only would.

Suddenly, as if discouraged, she rose well above him. I held my breath, for I knew what was coming. The little fellow stood on the edge of the nest, looking down at the plunge which he dared not take. There was a sharp cry from behind, which made him alert, tense as a watch spring. The next instant the mother eagle swooped, striking the nest at his feet, sending his support of twigs and himself with them out into the air.

He was afloat now, afloat on the blue air in spite of himself, and he flapped lustily for life. Over him, under him, beside him hovered the mother on tireless wings, calling softly that she was there. But the awful fear of the depths and the lance tops of the spruces was upon the little one; his flapping grew more wild; he fell faster and faster. Suddenly—more in fright, it seemed to me, than because he had spent his strength—he lost his balance and tipped head downward in the air. It was all over now; he folded his wings to be dashed in pieces among the trees. Then like a flash the old mother eagle shot under him; his despairing feet touched her broad shoulders, between her wings. He righted himself, rested an instant, found his head; then she dropped like a shot from under him, leaving him to come down on his own wings. A handful of feathers, torn out by his claws, hovered slowly down after them.

For an instant I lost them among the trees far below. And when I found them again with my glass, the eaglet was in the top of a great pine and the mother was feeding him.

Then, standing there alone in the great wilderness, it flashed upon me for the first time just what the wise old prophet meant: "As an eagle stirreth up her nest, fluttereth over her young, spreadeth abroad her wings, taketh them, beareth them on her wings: So the Lord."

Little Thunder-Maker

TO one of our Indian tribes the ruffed grouse is known as *Sek-sah-ga-dah-gee*, "Little Thunder-Maker," because his spring drum call is like a faint rumble of distant thunder. It is a weirdly mysterious sound, as if a great heart were somewhere throbbing.

Any woodsman hearing it will say that a cock grouse is calling an unseen mate, but he will search many times in vain before finding the bird. His drumming is decidedly ventriloquial in that it seems to be everywhere, nowhere, and fades away into silence even as you turn your head to find out where it comes from. It is likewise one of the few fargoing sounds of nature which, like the hunting call of the great horned owl and the mourn of a timber wolf, never rouses an echo. Woodpeckers also sound the drums of spring, and if the drummer be a logcock the echo of his lusty *tat-a-tat* when he uses a dry stub as a drum, or his *dub-a-dub* when he uses a hollow tree, rebounds from hill to hill. But the drumming of a ruffed grouse comes and goes like the ghost of a sound that is felt rather than heard.

How does he drum? Widely different answers have been given, including one of mine that I now think was erroneous. "He beats a mossy log with his wings," says one observer, who forgets that precisely the same call is sent from a rock or the bare ground if no log is available. "He strikes his wings together over his back" is the conclusion of a second observer. "He beats his own sides with his wings," reports a third, who by patience and good luck has caught the drummer standing on tiptoe, framed by a blur which looks as if he had twenty wings whirring on each side.

In boyhood I became well acquainted with a cock grouse who had a drumming log at either end of his range. On an April morning when he was drumming from one log I hid near the other and thumped a blown bladder that was buttoned under my jacket, increasing the speed from a slow *brum brum* to a long roll, just as I had heard the drum call many times. Hardly had it ceased before the old grouse darted in and pulled himself up, so near that I could see the angry glint of his hazel eye. He probably thought that some cheeky young cock had dared to drum on his range, on his own log, and his strut-strutting was that of a game rooster who hears a rival crowing. Since he mistook my thumping for a drum call, naturally I concluded that he drummed by beating his own sides, but from a much later observation I drew a different and much more probable conclusion.

On a ridge behind my spring fishing camp on Moosehead Lake I had heard a drum call several times by day and once on a moonlit night. I traced it to a little opening, halfway up the ridge, carpeted by dead beech leaves and curtained on all sides but one by thickets of fir and spruce. In the middle of this opening was a hardwood log, not mossy but dry as a bone, and on it was a single grouse feather. At first I waited for a drum call before beginning my stalk; but despite all woodcraft the drummer saw or heard me and vanished, not with the explosive whir that usually marks his take-off but gliding away silently, close to the ground, as if the drumming log, too, must be kept secret from prying eyes.

On my next attempt, having noted the hour of his performance, I was hidden under a low-branching fir on the open side of the stage when the thunder-maker came mincing into sight, frequently stopping to look and listen on all sides. He was a shy actor, and his senses must have been extraordinarily keen. Not until he was satisfied that he had the stage all to himself did he hop lightly to the log and parade up and down, drooping his wing tips, opening his lustrous ruff, spreading wide his handsome tail.

Facing me at last, while I held my breath, he raised both wings to strike them forward and downward with a motion too fast for eyes to follow, and the tense silence of the woods was broken by a single low *brum*. Other wing beats followed, the tempo increasing until the separate beats merged into a continuous roll, which suddenly and mysteriously tapered away into silence. The mystery was, and still is, that the sound grows faint while the wings are still threshing rapidly.

After seeing the performance a second time, my impression was that the wings do not strike over his back or beat against his sides. On the downward stroke they stop before coming together, and the *brum* is made, I think, by columns of compressed air striking together, just as thunder itself may possibly be made by air rushing into the vacuum produced by a lightning bolt.

In an effort to observe this at closer range, I went early one morning to become part of the scenery, having convinced myself by a thousand experiments that wild eyes are sensitive to motion but indifferent to form or color that remains absolutely still. The drummer usually appeared near one end of his log, so I sat on the ground at the other end, after giving my clothes a mottled appearance by a sprinkling of dead leaves and bits of moss to become an inconspicuous part of the forest floor. When at last the drummer appeared, gliding onto the stage from under a bending fir tip, I had become one with his drumming log; my eyes were half closed to hood their telltale lights, old gray hat pulled low, shoulders limply hunched, hands in my lap half hidden by a spray of moosewood leaves.

Thunder-Maker was now out of sight, but I heard a tiny thump when he jumped up on the log and a fainter scratch of toes as he paraded in my direction. Close beside my bent head he stopped, so near that one could feel the presence of an intensely animate thing. A long silence, which may have been two seconds or two minutes, was followed by an elflike sound of little feet moving away, halting, coming back. Then came a low thump on the ground, a rustle like a whisper, and Thunder-Maker was gone under the same drop curtain that marked his entrance.

No, he did not drum, but he gave me an unforgettable moment when he stood at my shoulder, looking with surprise at my old hat and perhaps wondering at the queer mushroom that had grown overnight on his drumming log.

Ornithologists have called our little thunder-maker *Bonasa* because, they say, the whir of his wings when rising from the ground is like the roar of *Bonasus*, the wild ox. It is a startling sound, louder and more explosive than his drumming, but for some reason beyond my ken it does not carry nearly so far. On a still day you can hear Thunder-Maker at a distance of a quarter mile or so (once I measured it at over two hundred paces), but you would have to strain your ears to hear his wild-ox roar at forty yards. The sound is heard only for a second or less, after which he speeds away on silent wings and often rocks himself cradlewise, left-right, especially when going fast with the wind under his tail. It is a beautifully rhythmic flight, like poetry in swift motion.

Since Thunder-Maker jumps almost instantly into high gear, it is possible that the roaring is simply the result of stiff wings in rapid vibration; but I think, on the contrary, that it is caused by a voluntary twist of the outer wing quills, as a nighthawk booms, and that he does it purposely to frighten or fluster an enemy. The proof is that he can rise from the ground as quietly as any other large bird except an owl when he so pleases.

On an autumn day, while roaming the Redding hills to see how the grouse were faring, I went down into a woodsy hollow where formerly one might find a whole covey of grouse feeding on the glossy leaves and crimson fruit of wintergreen or checkerberry plants. A solitary grouse roared up, to speed out of the woods and away over a bare knoll, as if bound for distant cover. Following his line of flight, I was climbing the knoll when my eye caught a faint motion by a stone on the rounded crest; and there was my grouse, huddled down to make himself a part of the gray-brown earth, so well concealed that any careless eye would overlook him. Giving him a wide berth, I sauntered on a few steps before stopping to look far ahead, as if for my vanished game, while all my faculties were centered behind me. At a faint stir I whirled to see the grouse speeding on silent wings back to the feeding ground from which he had just been driven.

This little adventure, which has been often repeated with variations, brings to mind one of Thunder-Maker's characteristic traits. So long as he thinks himself unseen he will hold quiet while you pass by; but the moment you stop, or change your saunter to a quickstep, he thinks you have discovered him and is away on what may be either a roaring or a quiet flight, as he himself determines. In just the same way I have seen a young buck bound away at sight or scent of danger, or an old buck lift his antlered head above cover to watch a hunter pass and then lie down in the same day bed. In one case the action is purely instinctive; in the other, instinct is modified by individual will or purpose or intelligence.

From the manner of Thunder-Maker's take-off it is sometimes possible to judge where he will make a landing. If he rises high on a parabolic flight he usually holds a fairly straightaway course for a hundred yards or so and then swings to right or left and planes down to earth again. If his take-off is low he usually ends a short flight by slanting up into a tree, preferably an evergreen, as a refuge from enemies. Occasionally but rarely he lights lengthwise of a big limb and huddles down to become like a formless growth of moss or fungus; more often he lights on a small limb, close to the trunk, and there, stretching his neck and snugging down his feathers, makes himself look like a dead stub. Unless your eyes are trained, you may go around the tree and search its every branch without finding what you look for. If you want to discover where Thunder-Maker hides, sit down at a little distance and hold still. At this waiting game no bird or animal has the patience or self-control of a man; you have only to keep quiet and your game, whatever it may be, will make the first betraying move.

Sportsmen, who have written the most and best about Thunder-Maker because they regard him as the king of game birds, have a tradition which says that a flushed grouse always gets quickly behind a tree as a safety play against being shot. That he usually gets behind a tree is true, beyond doubt; but how, one may reasonably ask, could he possibly do anything else? When he sees you coming straight at him he takes a few quick steps to get out of sight before he explodes into the air. Trees are in front of him, not one but many, and he must either go through them or around them. Having too much sense to break his neck by speeding into an obstacle, he naturally whips around it and so puts a tree behind him, as the books all tell with wonder at such cunning.

Because of his still pinions, Thunder-Maker is so careless of small obstacles that after he is in the air and out of sight you often hear a click, click as his wing quills hit a twig or leaf; but any mourning dove would follow the same swift course without touching a thing. Other woodland birds have discovered another way of flying through thick cover. Take the jumping flight of a woodpecker or the undulating flight of a goldfinch as an example of how flying birds fold their wings and let their momentum carry them through a small opening. I once saw a goldfinch in full flight go through a woven-wire fence with a four-inch mesh; by closing his wings at precisely the right instant and right distance he bounced through a selected opening without touching a wire on either side. If nature had given Thunder-Maker such a gift he might slip through the branches of a maple or a pine instead of whipping around the whole tree, and so give the baffled sportsman a better occasion to wonder at such cunning.

After a lifetime of rather intimate acquaintance, to me the wildness of Thunder-Maker is still his most fascinating trait. He is a child of the wilderness, and so long as one of his kind lives in our sadly diminished woods his mottled colors, swift-gliding walk, and thunderous flight will recall the sights and sounds and wordless feel of the solitude where only he feels at home.

In my boyhood, when grouse were plentiful, I could always find two or three nests within a half mile of the farmhouse; season after season I followed the chicks from the time they chipped the shell until late October, when each brood scattered widely and so met another brood for the first time. Naturally it was a temptation to tame such lovely little wildlings, as one made pets of certain downy bantam and Brahma chicks that had less distrust of humanity than others.

Near me lived a boy who had a genius for taming almost any wild thing, from toad or snake to a nestling crow or a young skunk, or a woodchuck dug out of a den. Every spring we would catch one chick, only one, from a grouse brood and do our best to tame him, but always in vain. The little wild thing would not touch food of any kind from our hand, not even ant grubs or fly grubs, which young grouse naturally eat with relish. When placed in a roomy cage with a ground floor of forest litter he would spend every moment until he died in trying to find a way out. Or if, in despair, we put him in charge of a banty hen with chicks of her own, he vanished within the hour, never to be seen again. One captive chick, when placed at twilight under the mother banty with her chicks, darted out on the other side and headed straight for unseen woods as if he knew just where he came from.

The few people I know who have tried to raise grouse all tell the same disturbing story. They say that the young birds are moody, temperamental, quarrelsome—so anti-social, in fact, that they peck or chivvy or fight one another, and in this respect the hens are more temperamental than the cocks.

I have observed only one such brood of hand-raised grouse, which was hatched on a game farm from a clutch of wild eggs after a gray fox had killed the setting mother bird. That they were moody, quarrelsome, and in most other respects very different from wild grouse was plainly evident, but there are, I think, two reasons to account for their anti-social action. The first is that they instinctively resented the artificiality of the whole thing: the confinement, the wire-screened flooring of their small run, the frequent checks when a man appeared and they could not follow their instinctive urge to escape an enemy by hiding or running. Above all, it was this lack of liberty, which is the one thing that every natural creature wants and that a grouse must have to be content with his lot. The strongest instinct in him—stronger than the urge for food or for self-protection—is his instinct for freedom.

The second and more inclusive reason for the moody conduct in captivity is that there is no mother grouse to give orders to her young. Any man who follows a brood in the wild soon learns that the mother is constantly talking to them, and that the chicks respond to her every word or signal. At one sound they go cheeping contently over a feeding ground; at another, they gather close about the mother in silence; at a third, they disappear as if the ground had opened to cover them. To every signal they are responsive but free creatures, obedient only to the mother's warning and their own will. Men have slowly learned how to care for chickens or pheasants or even quail, but Little Thunder-Maker is a different bird. Wildness is born in him, and if ever we are to restock our empty covers we must somehow find a substitute for his training or instruction by a mother grouse during his formative months.

All this is more or less theoretical, but, as a plain matter of observation, there is nothing moody or temperamental in the many broods of young grouse I have met here in long-settled New England or in the wilderness around my northern camp-grounds where, untroubled by men or dogs, they are wholly natural. It is a joy to hear the low, inquiring *kwit-kwit* of a mother grouse and the eager answering *prrt, prrt*, which seems to say, "Here am I," as eight or ten chicks respond one after another. This is their way of keeping in touch while they twist their separate ways among thick-growing alders or through a sprangle of ferns where an unresponsive chick would quickly go astray and be lost. It is even more fascinating to meet them at sundown, when with full crops they wander leisurely toward the roosting place in a leafy thicket. Their voices are now less eager, more sleepy; but still they are talking to the mother bird or with one another, and to my ears it sounds like happy talk.

Each of these wild broods keeps to its own small range during the long summer. In autumn they begin to scatter and meet members of another brood on a new feeding ground where late mushrooms are springing or beechnuts falling. Aside from momentary tiffs over a difference of opinion, I have never seen a grouse quarreling either with his own family group or with the strangers of another group. In the early spring, before the first drum calls roll through the woods, I have repeatedly observed a number of grouse, sometimes four or five, occasionally double that number, gathered on a southern slope where melting snow has bared the first patch of ground with its penetrating earthy smell. Always there were both sexes in the group, as one could fairly well judge by the larger ruff, more perfectly banded tail, and brighter color of the cock bird.

Once, after eight full-grown grouse had stood quietly awhile, as if getting acquainted, they joined in a kind of ceremonial performance, moving in and out with raised crests and drooping wings in a dance like an old-fashioned minuet. At intervals in the stately play came an interlude: one or other of the cocks would walk to the center of the stage to bob his head and turn around and around on his toes like a pigeon, but silently, without a word from any of the company. When such a party broke up, the grouse moved quietly away on foot, not all together but in two or three directions, which meant that they were returning each to his own home range.

During the long spring and summer months that young grouse spend with the mother bird they acquire habits which are as regularly repeated as the rounds of a postman, and as close to the hour as a good clock. They feed for two or three hours in the morning; they preen or dust themselves or just loaf for an equal time at noon; in the afternoon they feed again and, toward sundown, move leisurely toward the roosting place.

Their food varies with the season—buds, tender leaves, grubs, insects, fruit, berries, seeds, mushrooms, beechnuts, acorns—but at all seasons they like a variety and go from one feeding ground to another, not haphazardly but in regular sequence. If you know where wild grapes are ripening, be assured that every covey of grouse in the neighborhood also knows it, and that they will eat grapes at about the same time every morning. They like buckwheat better than any other grain, and if you know of a field of ripe buckwheat near the woods you may confidently expect to find grouse there in the late afternoon.

Fruit is quickly digested and has comparatively little nourishment, while grain and other seeds have good staying power, but it may be only a coincidence that you find grouse on a wild grapevine in the morning, or that in the late afternoon, with a long night ahead, you find them in a buckwheat field.

When wild raspberries ripen it is holiday time for all grouse, but here again they seem to regard fruit as a morning diet. At first they pick up every overripe berry that has fallen to the ground; then they look with longing at the abundance beyond reach. They cannot fly up to it because the cover is too dense for wings, and their feet—with stout toes in front and only an apology for a toe behind—were designed for walking, not for perching or climbing. Two or three young birds make a brave attempt by jumping on a slanting stalk, and their weight bends it to an easier slant. Awkwardly they hitch their way up sidewise, higher, higher, until a red-ripe berry is within reach; and usually, in an overeager attempt to reach it, they lose balance and tumble off, only to try the same vine again. Meanwhile the old mother has selected a heavy-laden vine and tapped it smartly with a stiffened wing. A few of the ripest berries are shaken off, and now the whole covey is just a mass of bobbing gray-brown backs and cheeping voices as they glean the fallen berries before scattering to find a better harvest.

When all ground food is hidden under snow, Little Thunder-Maker has one advantage over quail, pheasants, and other birds of the same ornithological family. In the late afternoon he flies up into a birch or wild apple tree, there to fill his crop with next summer's leaf buds, which are already formed and filled with nourishment that needs no sand or gravel to help grind it up and make it digestible. I have twice found a whole covey of quail dead under the snow; dissection revealed that they had found enough weed seeds to keep them alive, but not a bit of necessary gravel. We can only wonder why nature gave this gift of bud feeding to Thunder-Maker alone, or how he discovered it for himself.

A surprising thing about Thunder-Maker's feeding habits came to light one autumn when I asked three or four sportsmen to bring me the crop contents of every grouse they shot, and one of them brought a crop stuffed with sweet acorns. The surprise was that every acorn was shelled and quartered; there was not a scrap of outer covering in the whole handful. I knew that this kind of acorn had a hard shell with a pointed top, and how Thunder-Maker shelled it so neatly with his beak puzzled me completely, nor could any naturalist of my acquaintance give me the answer.

Two or three years later, while I was roaming through autumn woods, a loud rustling of leaves froze me in my tracks. No animate thing was in sight, but the rustling went on with intervals of silence, until it was located on the other side of a lichen-covered stone wall. Creeping on hands and knees, I peeked between two rocks; and there was a big grouse, plainly a cock, scratching among the oak leaves. New-fallen acorns were visible on both sides of the wall, and with elation I thought, "Now at last I shall see how he does it."

Thunder-Maker's answer to the puzzle made me feel foolish, remembering my own cut fingers when I had tried to shell these nuts. He was digging out *old* acorns, which had lain for a year under moist leaves, softened by rain and frost. A few whacks of his bill took off the shell; another whack split the ivory-colored meat into halves and quarters. In a wild grape-vine thicket I had seen him swallow a whole grape, as big as the end of my thumb, which would lose half its nourishment if broken open, and had watched with fascination as it moved slowly down his slim neck, like an orange forced into a child's Christmas stocking. Here in the open oak woods behind the old gray wall he was shelling and quartering acorns which he swallowed quite easily.

Besides four or five regular feeding grounds and a favorite opening where he suns himself after rain, Little Thunder-Maker has at least one place to which he resorts when his morning hunger is satisfied. To it come at noon all members of his covey or family group, there to preen themselves or to gossip awhile. This loafing place of grouse is always in some out-of-the-way corner where hunters with their bird dogs seldom or never look; which explains why one may unexpectedly flush two or three or a dozen of these splendid game birds after tramping all morning through empty covers.

There was one such loafing place where, in years past, I met literally scores of grouse but never a man or even a boy. It was a lonely hilltop, thickly covered with steeple-shaped cedars; here and there were little openings where the sun shown warmly and no chill November wind ever entered. The cedars are still there, some of the grouse, too, and it is happily the safest kind of a place because the sportsman has no chance to use his gun. As you slip quietly through the cover your eye catches an alert motion ahead, close to the ground. So long as you hold still you see and hear nothing; but at your next forward step comes the whirring, nerve-tingling rise which tells that an unseen covey of grouse is up and away.

In going from one feeding ground to the next in order, and

from the morning feeding ground to the loafing place at noon, every grouse follows the same course. He goes leisurely on foot if he feels at ease, or swiftly by air if flushed by an enemy. He has definite paths through the cover, as a fox has runways, although they are as invisible to human eyes as his regular flyways. Day after day he holds to the same footways and flyways because he formed the habit when, as a helpless chick, he followed the wise old mother bird in the same cover. With one exception he seems to know at any moment where to go or what to do next, and so keeps his wits ever ready for an emergency.

In my native southern New England, as elsewhere, poachers took advantage of this regularity of habit to bring grouse dangerously near to extinction. They would build a low fence of brush and litter, only a few inches high, across a whole feeding ground; at intervals of four or five yards was a narrow opening framed by two sticks stuck in the ground, and at every opening a wire noose was set at the height that a grouse carries his head. Coming to this unexpected obstacle, a surprised grouse would walk along it to find an opening and put his neck in the noose. Tens of thousands of the grandest of game birds were thus strangled, choked by their desperate effort to break loose, and were sold in our city markets. In a lifetime I have kicked to pieces I know not how many brush fences and carried away the wires, and I have gone back to repeat the lesson if a second were needed.

At first glance it looks incredible that a bird as keen as Thunder-Maker should walk along a fence that he could easily step over or put his life in peril by walking into a trap, but lifelong habits are hard for any creature to change. All natural creatures live by instinctive faith, expecting no evil today where yesterday they found good; that is why Thunder-Maker puts his head into a wire noose, not being able to imagine what a noose is for, thinking it is only a bent stem of grass. Hares, bobcats, foxes, even the timber wolf, wariest and most intelligent of animals, put their heads into a snare set over runways where they have always walked in safety.

The exception to Thunder-Maker's regularity, which tells him where to go at any hour or what to do in any emergency, comes when you fluster him suddenly by appearing at a moment when he has no warning of your presence in the woods. Several times, when sitting motionless in the woods, he has come near enough for me to touch him. Ordinarily he comes and goes without alarm, but once when I reached out a hand for him he was thrown completely off balance. He jumped back, stumbled over a root, whirled around, and then remembered his wings long enough to seek refuge in a spruce tree. He flew in a direction opposite to the way he had been going, which was proof enough of his wandering wits, for, whether walking or flying, a grouse holds to his course until driven to the limit of his range, when he will roar up in your face and whip over your head, speeding back to where he feels at home.

Although Thunder-Maker will come near to you in full daylight, the only time you can come close to him is in the dark, after he has settled down for the night. Until the snow falls a solitary grouse, especially a cock, usually sleeps on the ground, huddled against a brown stump where he becomes a bit of the sleeping earth. Once, when following an old lumber road in the dusk, I somehow knew that a stump which stood among many stumps beside the trail was a living thing. But what? Even when bending over it, after catfooting within range, my eyes could make out nothing but form or bulk. Not until I touched it did Thunder-Maker roar up in my face, giving me a bigger scare than he had.

Another time, in the twilight, I recognized Thunder-Maker as he slept on his feet against a lichen-covered rock. Taking plenty of time, I moved in, stood for a moment near enough to see that his eyes were open, and backed slowly away, leaving him undisturbed. Evidently he feels safe when he goes to sleep, thinking himself so well concealed or camouflaged by his natural surroundings that no eye will recognize him. I think, also, that any bird or animal, excepting a flesh eater, gives off little or no scent after he has been motionless for a few moments.

To winter cold, even to sub-zero cold, he is completely immune, thanks to his double coat of outer and inner feathers. On a stormy night he leaves his usual winter roost in a thick evergreen to dive into the snow, where he drives a down-slanting tunnel and turns around to make a little bedroom; but that, I think, is not so much to escape the cold as to get out of the pelting, snow-laden wind—perhaps, also, to hide where his worst enemy, the great horned owl, never even looks for him.

A memorable example of how even a mother grouse, more wary than Thunder-Maker, may be flustered by an unexpected appearance was given me, one September day, in an alder swamp of the Maine woods. A faintly marked trail ran past my feet; to the left was a deep, dark brook, bridged by a mossy log—a treacherous crossing. I was listening for the repetition of a queer animal cry that had puzzled me when a grouse came gliding down the trail, heading for the log bridge and followed by eight or ten well-grown chicks. She did not notice me, and on an impulse of curiosity, just to see what she might do, I stepped out in front of her, blocking the way.

A mother grouse habitually reacts to such an alarm by throw-

ing herself at your feet, whining, floundering, and dragging a
broken wing, to hold your attention while her chicks scatter
and hide. One goes under a dun leaf, another into a tuft of
brown grass, a third huddles beside a dark root; and there they
hold motionless, their bright eyes closed, as if they know how
to make themselves invisible by becoming a part of the forest
floor.

But this mother grouse and her brood were apparently too
flustered to use their natural wits. At the sight of a strange
animal, they tumbled over one another, forgetting they had
wings in their haste to run quickly out of sight. For a full
minute they were silent as if listening, then a low talking began, with questions and answers, as I backed silently behind
a thick alder clump. At an insistent kind of note, or so it
sounded in my ear, the talking ceased. In a moment the mother
bird appeared, her head high; into the trail behind her flowed
from either side a rill of bobbing feathers. Once more I stepped
out to block the way and again the whole brood vanished, to
be silent a moment and then to talk about this strange animal
that bothered without harming them.

The comedy ended in a surprising way when the mother
gave me a piece of her mind. Out she came like a little fury,
ruffling up her feathers, quivering her wings, and squealing—
yes, *squealing*—a protest at my unmannerly ways. As if frightened by her demonstrations I drew hastily back, and on the
instant she scooted over the log bridge with the whole brood
stringing close on her heels. There was a winking of alder leaves
on the other side of the brook, and they were gone.

An Oriole's Nest

THERE is the nest, swinging through sunlight and the shadow of the old elm boughs! It is a delightful cradle for the young orioles, swayed all day long by the summer breeze; the little ones peep through chinks as the world sweeps by, and whistle cheerily as they are blown high or low with never a fear of falling. The mother bird must feel very comfortable about them as she goes off caterpillar hunting, for no enemy can trouble the little ones while she is gone. The blacksnake, that horror of all low-nesting birds, will never climb so high. The red squirrel cannot find a footing on those delicate branches. Neither can the crow find a resting place from which to steal the young; and the hawk's legs are not long enough to reach down and grasp them, if he should venture near the house.

The oriole is a neighborly little body, and that helps her.

Although the young are kept from harm anywhere by the cunning instinct which builds a hanging nest, she still prefers to build near a house, where hawks and crows and owls rarely come. She knows her friends and takes advantage of their protection, returning year after year to the same old elm, and, like a thrifty housewife, she carefully saves and sorts the good threads of her storm-wrecked old house to be used in building a new one.

But recently the pretty nests on the secluded streets of New England towns are growing scarcer. The orioles are peace-loving birds, and dislike the society of those noisy, pugnacious little rascals, the English sparrows, which have taken possession of our streets. Often now I find the nests far away from any house, on lonely roads where, a few years ago, they were rarely seen. Sometimes a solitary farmhouse, too far from the town to be much visited by sparrows, has two or three nests swinging from its old elms, where formerly there was but one.

It is interesting evidence of the bird's keen instinct that, on lonely roads and away from houses, the nests are noticeably deeper and so better protected from bird enemies. The same thing is occasionally noticed of nests built in maple or apple trees, which are without the protection of drooping branches upon which birds of prey can find no footing. Some wise birds assure themselves of the same protection by simply contracting the neck of the nest, instead of building a deep one. Young birds, building their first nests, seem afraid to trust in the strength of their own weaving. Their nests are invariably shallow, and so suffer most from birds of prey.

In the choice of building material the birds are very careful. They know that no branch supports the nest from beneath and that the safety of the young orioles depends on good material,

well woven together. In some wise way they seem to know at a
glance whether a thread is strong enough to be trusted; but
sometimes, in selecting the first threads that are to bear the
whole weight of the nest, they are unwilling to rely on appearances. At such times a pair of birds may be seen holding a
tug of war; they stand with feet braced, shaking and pulling
the thread like a pair of terriers, until it is well tested.

In gathering and proving the materials for a nest, the orioles
display no little ingenuity. One day I was lying under some
shrubs, watching a pair of birds that were building close to the
house. It was a typical nest-making day. The sun was bright
through the delicate green leaves and a glory of white apple
blossoms; the air was filled with warmth and fragrance, and
birds and bees were busy everywhere. Orioles always seem
happy; this day they quite overflowed in the midst of all the
brightness, even though materials were scarce and they had to
be diligent.

The female was very industrious, never returning to the nest
without some contribution; the male frolicked about the trees
in his brilliant orange and black, whistling his warm rich notes,
and looking like a dash of sunshine amid the blossoms. Sometimes he stopped his frolic to find a bit of string, over which
he raised an impromptu jubilate; once in a while he flew with
his mate to the nest, uttering that soft rich twitter of his in a
mixture of blarney and congratulation whenever she found
some particularly choice material. But his chief part seemed
to be to furnish the celebration, while she took care of the work.

In front of me, under the lee of the old wall where some
line-stripping gale had blown it, there was a torn fragment of
cloth with loose threads showing everywhere. I was wondering

why the birds did not use it, when the male, in one of his lively flights, discovered it and flew down. First he hopped all around it; next he tried some threads; but, as the cloth was lying loose on the grass, the whole piece came whenever he pulled. For a few moments he worked diligently, trying a pull on each side in succession. Once he tumbled end over end in a comical scramble, when the fragment caught on a grass stub which gave way when he had braced himself and was pulling hardest. He abruptly flew off, and I thought he had given up the attempt.

But in a minute he was back with his mate, thinking, no doubt, that she, as a capable little manager, would know all about such things. The two worked together for some minutes, getting an occasional thread, but not enough to pay for the labor. The trouble was that they both pulled together on the same side, so they merely dragged the bit of cloth all over the lawn, instead of getting out the threads they wanted. Once they unraveled a long thread by pulling at right angles, but the next moment they were together on the same side again. The male seemed to do not as he was told, but exactly what he saw his mate do. Whenever she pulled at a thread, he hopped around, as close to her as he could get, and pulled too.

Twice they had given up the attempt, only to return after hunting futilely elsewhere. I was wondering how long their patience would last, when the female suddenly seized the cloth by a corner and flew along close to the ground, dragging it after her, chirping loudly all the while. She disappeared into a hawthorn tree in a corner of the garden, where the male followed her a moment later.

Curious about what they were doing, yet afraid of disturbing them, I waited where I was until I saw both birds fly to the nest, each with some long threads. This was repeated; and my curiosity got the better of me. While the orioles were weaving the last threads into their nest, I ran round the house, crept a long way behind the old wall to a safe hiding place near the hawthorn.

The orioles had solved their problem; the piece of cloth was fastened there securely among the thorns. Soon the birds came back, seized some threads by the ends, and raveled them out without difficulty. It was the work of but a moment to gather as much material as they could use at one weaving. For an hour or more I watched them working industriously at the hawthorn and the old elm, where the nest was growing rapidly to a beautiful depth. Several times the bit of cloth slipped from the thorns as the birds pulled upon it, but as often as it did they carried it back and fastened it more securely, until at last it grew so snarled that they could get no more long threads and they left it for good.

That same day I carried out some bright-colored bits of worsted and ribbon and scattered them on the grass. The birds soon found them and used them in completing their nest. For a while a gayer little dwelling was never seen in a tree. The bright bits of color in the soft gray of the walls gave the nest a holiday appearance in keeping with the high spirits of the orioles. But by the time the young had chipped the shell and the joyousness of nest building had given place to the constant duties of filling hungry little mouths, the rains and the sun of summer had bleached the bright colors to a uniform sober gray.

That was a happy family from beginning to end. No accident ever befell it; no enemy disturbed its peace. And when the young birds had flown away to the South, I took down the nest which I had helped to build, and hung it in my study as a souvenir of my bright little neighbors.

Whitooweek, the Hermit

WHITOOWEEK, the woodcock, the strangest hermit in all the woods, is a bird of mystery. Only the hunters know anything about him, and to the hunters, who are practically his only human acquaintances, he is a game bird pure and simple; their interest is chiefly in his death. He hides the details of his daily life, from them and from all others, in the dark woods where he spends all the sunny hours and in the soft twilight when he stirs abroad, like an owl, after his long day's rest. Of a hundred farmers on whose lands I have found Whitooweek or the signs of his recent feeding, scarcely five knew from observation that such a bird existed, so well does he play the hermit under our very noses.

The reasons for this are many. By day he rests on the ground in some dark bit of cover, by a brown stump that exactly matches his feathers or in a tangle of dead leaves and brakes where it is almost impossible to see him. At such times his strange fearlessness of man helps to hide him, for he will let you pass within a few feet of him without stirring. That is partly because he sees poorly by day and perhaps does not realize how near you are, and partly because he knows that his soft colors hide him so well amidst his surroundings that you cannot see him, however near you come. This confidence of his is well placed; once I saw a man step over a brooding woodcock on her nest in the roots of an old stump without seeing her, and she never moved so much as the tip of her long bill as he passed. In the late twilight when woodcocks first stir abroad there is only a shadow which passes swiftly across a bit of clear sky as Whitooweek goes off to the meadow brook to feed, or there is a rustle in the alders as he turns the dead leaves over, and a faint *peeunk*, like the voice of a distant nighthawk. Then you catch a glimpse of a shadow that flits along the ground, with a weaving, batlike flutter of wings as you draw near to investigate. No wonder, under such circumstances, that Whitooweek passes all his summers and raises brood upon brood of downy invisible chicks in a farmer's wood lot without ever being found out or recognized.

My own acquaintance with Whitooweek began when I was a child. I had no name to give the strange bird that I watched day after day, and those whom I asked for information laughed at my description and said no such bird existed. Just beyond the upland pasture on the northern slopes there were some dark, wet maple woods, and beyond that the ground slanted away through scrub and alders to a little wild meadow where cowslips grew beside the brook. One April day, as I was stealing through the maple woods, I stopped suddenly at seeing something shining like a jewel almost at my feet. It was an eye, a bird's eye, but it was some moments before I could realize that it was really a bird sitting there on her nest between the broken ends of an old stub that had fallen years ago.

I backed away quietly and knelt down to watch the queer find. Her bill was enormously long and straight, and her eyes were away up at the back of her head—that was my first observation. A wandering horse had put his hoof down and made a hollow in the dry rotten wood of the fallen stub. Into this hollow a few leaves and brown grass stems had been gathered —a careless kind of nest, yet serving its purpose wonderfully, for it hid the brooding mother so well that it would be possible to step on her without ever knowing that bird or nest was near.

I went away quietly that day and left her undisturbed; and I remember perfectly that I took with me something of the wonder and something, too, of the fear, with which a child naturally meets a wild thing for the first time. That she should be so still and fearless before me was a perfect argument to a child that she had some hidden means of defense—the long bill, perhaps, or a hidden sting—with which it was not well to trifle. All that seems very strange and far away to me now, but it was real enough then to a very small boy, alone in the dark woods, who met for the first time a large bird with an enormously long bill and eyes on the back of her head where they plainly did not belong, a bird moreover that had no fear and seemed perfectly well able to take care of herself.

The next day I came back again. The strange bird was there on her nest as before, her long bill resting over the edge of the hollow and looking at first glance like a twig. She showed no fear whatever, and, encouraged at her quietness and assurance,

I crept nearer and nearer until with my finger I touched her bill and turned it gently aside. At this she wiggled it impatiently, and I discovered that the tip of the upper bill is flexible and can be moved about almost like the tip of a finger. At the same time she uttered a curious hissing sound that frightened me again and made me think of snakes and hidden stings, so I drew back and watched her from a safe distance. She sat perfectly motionless, with only an occasional turning of the long bill. Once when she had been still a very long time, I turned her head aside again, and to my astonishment and delight she made no objection but left her head as I had turned it, and presently she let me twist it back again. After her first warning she seemed to understand the situation perfectly, and had no concern for the wondering child who watched her and who had no intention whatever of harming her or her nest.

Others had laughed at my description of a brown bird with a long bill and eyes at the back of her head, so I said no more to them, but at the first opportunity I hunted up Natty Dingle and told him all about it. Natty was a gentle, improvident little man, who would never do any hard work for pay but would cheerfully half kill himself to go fishing through the ice or to oblige a neighbor. Most of his time in pleasant weather he spent in roaming about the woods, or fishing lazily and catching fish where no one else could ever get them. He knew all about the woods, knew every bird and beast and plant, and one boy at least, to my knowledge, would rather go with him for a day's fishing than see the president's train or go to a circus.

Unlike the others, Natty did not laugh at my description but listened patiently and told me I had found a woodcock's nest—a rare thing, he said, for though he had roamed the woods so much and shot hundreds of the birds in season, he had never yet seen a nest. He went with me, and as we rounded the end of the fallen stub the woodcock's confidence deserted her and she slipped away noiselessly into the leafy shadows. Then we saw her four eggs, very big at one end, very little at the other, and beautifully colored and spotted.

Natty, who was wise in his way, merely glanced at the nest and then drew me aside into hiding, and before we knew it or had even seen her approach, Mother Woodcock was brooding her eggs again. Then Natty, who had doubted one part of my story, whispered to me to go out; the bird never stirred as I crept near on hands and knees and touched her as before.

A few minutes later we crept away, and Natty took me to the swamp to show me the borings. We found them in plenty wherever the earth was soft—numerous holes, as if made with a pencil, where the woodcock had probed the earth with her long bill. She was hunting for slugs and soft beetles and delicate white grubs. Woodcocks hunt by scent and feeling, and also by listening for the slight sounds made by the worms underground, Natty told me, and that is why the eyes are far back on the head, to be out of the way and also to watch for danger above and behind while the bird's bill is deep in the mud. That also explains why the tip of the bill is flexible, so that when the bird bores in the earth and has failed to locate the game accurately by hearing, the sensitive tip of the bill feels around until it finds and seizes the morsel.

When I went back to the spot a few days later, the nest was deserted. A few bits of shell scattered about told me that I must now hunt for the little woodcocks, which are almost impossible to find unless the mother herself shows you where they are. A week later, as I prowled along the edge of the swamp, a sudden little brown whirlwind seemed to roll up the leaves at my feet. In the midst of it I made out the woodcock fluttering away, clucking, and trailing now a wing and now a leg, as if desperately hurt. Of course I followed her to see what was the matter. When she had led me to a safe distance all her injuries vanished as at the touch of magic. She sprang up on strong wings, whirled across the swamp and circled swiftly back to where I had first started her. But I did not find one of the little woodcocks, although I hunted for them half an hour, and they were probably hiding among the leaves and grass stems under my very eyes.

The little woodcocks, though scarcely bigger than bumble-bees, run about hardily, like young partridges, the moment they chip the shell, and they begin at once to learn from the mother where to look for food. In the early twilight, when they are less wild and the mother is not so quick to flutter away and draw you after her, I have sometimes surprised a brood of them— wee, downy, invisible things, each with a comically long bill and a stripe down his back that seems to divide the little fellow and hide one half of him even after you have discovered the other. The mother is always with them and leads them swiftly among the bogs and ferns and alder stems, where they turn over the dead leaves and shreds of wet bark with their bills for the grubs that hide beneath. Mother and chicks have a contented little twitter at such times that I have never heard under any other circumstances, which is probably intended to encourage each other and keep all the family within hearing as they run about in the twilight.

When the feeding grounds are far away from the nest, as is often the case, Whitooweek has two habits that are not found, I think, in any other game birds except perhaps the plover.

When food must be hunted for at a long distance, the mother will leave her brood in hiding and go herself to fetch it. When she returns she feeds the chicks, like a mother dove, by putting her bill in their throats and giving each his portion, going and coming until they are satisfied, when she leaves them in hiding again and feeds for herself during the rest of the night. Like most other young birds and animals who are left by their mothers, these never leave the spot where they have been told to stay, and they can hardly be driven away from it until the mother returns. Generally, when you find a brood of young woodcocks without the mother, they will let you pick them up and will lie as if dead in your hand, playing possum, until you put them down again.

When there is a good feeding ground near at hand, yet too far for the little chicks to travel, the mother will take them there, one by one, and hide them in a secret spot until she has brought the whole family. Two or three times I have seen woodcocks fly away with their young; once I saw a mother return to the spot from which, a few moments before, she had flown away with a chick and take another from under a leaf where I had not seen him. This curious method is used by the mothers not only to take the young to favorable feeding grounds, but also to get them quickly out of the way when there is danger from which it is impossible to hide.

So far as I can judge the process, which is always quickly done and extremely difficult to follow, the mother lights or walks directly over the chick and holds him between her knees as she flies. There are those who claim that the mother carries them in her bill, as a cat carries a kitten, but how that is possible without choking the little fellows is to me incomprehensible. The bill is not strong enough at the tip, I think, to hold

them by a wing, and to grasp them by the neck would, it seems
to me, most certainly suffocate or injure them in any prolonged
flight. Wild mothers generally handle their little ones with care.

There is another possible way in which Whitooweek may
carry her young, although I have never seen it. An old hunter
with whom I sometimes roamed the woods once stumbled
upon a mother woodcock and her brood by a little brook at the
foot of a wild hillside. One of the chicks was resting upon
the mother's back, just as one often sees a domestic chicken.
At my friend's sudden approach the mother rose, taking the
chick with her on her back, and vanished among the thick
leaves. The rest of the brood, three of them, disappeared instantly. I give the incident for what it is worth as a possible
suggestion, but I am quite sure that those that have come under my own observation were carried by an entirely different
method.

The young woodcocks begin to use their tiny wings within a
few days of leaving the eggs, earlier than young quail, and
they fly in a remarkably short time. Thanks to their good feeding, they grow with astonishing rapidity, so that often by early
summer the family scatters, each one to take care of himself,
leaving the mother free to raise another brood. At such times
they travel widely in search of food and come often into farm-
yards, spending half the night about the drains and stables
while the house is still. But they vanish at the first alarm, so
that Whitooweek is frequently a regular visitor in places where
he is never seen or suspected.

In his fondness for earthworms Whitooweek long ago
learned that it is much easier and simpler to pick up worms
than to dig for them. Earthworms stay on the surface of the
ground most of the night, and that is why the early bird *catches*

the worm, instead of digging him out, as the sleepy fellows must do. Midnight is the best time to get all the bait you want without trouble or worry. That is also the time when you are most likely to find Whitooweek at the same occupation, and often in a locality where no woodcocks are supposed to exist you will find, under the cabbage leaves or in the cool shade of the thick cornfield, the round holes where Whitooweek has been probing the soft earth for grubs and worms while you slept.

In the spring, while winning his mate, Whitooweek has one habit which reminds one instantly of the grass plovers of the open moors and uplands. Indeed, in his fondness for burned plains, where he can hide in plain sight and catch no end of grasshoppers and crickets without trouble, Whitooweek has many points in common with the almost unknown plovers. In the dusk, as you steal along the edge of the woods, you will hear a faint *peenk, peenk* close beside you, and as you turn to listen and locate the sound, a woodcock slants swiftly up over your head and begins to whirl in a spiral toward the heavens, clucking and twittering ecstatically. It is a poor kind of song, not to be compared with that of the grass plover, who does the same thing at twilight, and Whitooweek must help his voice by the clicking of his wings and by the humming of air through them, like the sharp voice of a reed in windy weather. But it sounds sweet enough, no doubt, to the little brown mate who is standing perfectly still near you, watching and listening to the performance.

At an enormous height, for him, Whitooweek whirls about madly for a few moments and then retraces his spiral downwards, clucking and twittering the while, until he reaches the treetops, where he folds his wings directly over his mate and drops like a plummet at her head. She still does not move, and when within a few feet of the ground Whitooweek spreads his wings wide to break his fall and drops quietly close beside her. There he remains for a moment, as if exhausted; but the next moment he is strutting about her, spreading wings and tail like a wild turkey gobbler, showing all his good points to the best advantage, and vain of all his performances as a peacock in the spring sunshine. Then he is quiet again; a faint *peent, peent* sounds, as if it were a mile away; and Whitooweek slants up on swift wings to repeat his ecstatic evolutions.

Both birds are strangely fearless of men at such times. If you keep still or move very softly, they pay no more attention to you than if you were one of the cattle cropping the first bits of grass close at hand. Like the golden plover, whose life is spent mostly in the vast solitudes of Labrador and Patagonia, they seem to have no instinctive fear of any large animal, and whatever fear Whitooweek has learned is the result of persistent hunting. Even in this he is slower to learn than any other game bird and when let alone for a season promptly returns to his native confidence.

When midsummer arrives a curious change comes over Whitooweek; the slight family ties are broken and the bird becomes a hermit for the rest of the year. He lives entirely alone, and not even in the migrating season does he join with his fellows in any large numbers, as most other birds do. No one, as far as I know, has ever seen anything that might be appropriately called a flock of woodcocks. The only exception to this rule is when, on rare occasions, a male woodcock is surprised strutting on a log, like a grouse, spreading wings and tail, and hissing and sputtering queerly as he moves up and down. Then it is possible to flush two or three other birds that may be watching beside the log or in the underbrush close at hand. One hunter told me that his setter had pointed a bird on a fallen log. The bird ceased his strutting as soon as he was discovered and slipped down into the ferns. When the dog drew nearer, five woodcocks flushed at the same moment, the greatest number found together that I have ever known.

With the beginning of the molt the birds desert the woods and swamps where they were reared and disappear absolutely. Where they go at this time is a profound mystery. In places where there were a dozen birds yesterday there are none today; and when you do stumble upon one it is generally in a spot where you never found one before, and where you will probably not find another, although you haunt the spot for years. This is the more remarkable in view of the fact that the woodcock, like most other birds, has certain favored spots to which he returns, to nest or feed or sleep, year after year.

Occasionally at this season you may find a solitary bird on a dry southern hillside or on the sunny edge of the big woods. He is pitiful to behold, having scarcely any feathers left to cover him, and he can only flutter or run away at your approach. If you have the rare fortune to surprise him when he does not see you, you will note a curious thing. He stands beside a stump or brake where the sun can strike his bare back fairly, as if he were warming himself. His long bill rests its tip on the ground, a prop supporting his head. He is asleep, but you will find that he sleeps with half an eye open. The lower lid seems to be raised until it covers half the eye; the upper half is clear, so that as he sleeps he can watch above and behind for his enemies. He gives out very little scent at such times, and a keen-nosed dog, which would wind him at a stone's throw in the autumn, will now pass close by without noticing him.

Hunters say that these scattered birds are those that have lost the most feathers, and that they keep to the sunny open spots for the sake of getting warm. Perhaps they are right, but what do these same birds do at night when the air is colder than by day? And, to contradict the theory, when there is one bird on a sunny open hillside, another may be a mile away, asleep in the heart of a big cornfield where the sun barely touches him the whole day long.

Whatever the reason for their action, these birds in July are rare, incomprehensible individuals. Whether they scatter widely to dense hiding places and by sitting close escape discovery or whether, like some of the snipe, they make a short northern migration in the molting season in search of solitude and a change of food, is yet to be discovered.

When the autumn comes you will notice another suggestion of the unknown plover in Whitooweek. Just as the plover arrives in the first heavy northeaster after August 20, so the first autumn moon that is obscured by heavy fog will surely bring the woodcock back to his accustomed haunts. But why he should wait for a full moon and then for a chill mist to cover it before beginning his southern flight is one of the mysteries. Unlike the plovers that come by the hundreds, Whitooweek slips in silent and solitary, and you go out in the morning, as to an appointment, to find him sleeping quietly just where you expected him to be.

With the first autumn flight another curious habit which comes out is that Whitooweek has a fondness for certain spots, not for any food or protection they give him, but evidently just from long association. Moreover, the scattered birds, in some unknown way, seem to keep account of the place, as if it were an inn, and as long as they remain in the neighborhood will often keep this one particular spot filled to its full complement.

Some three miles north of where I live there is a certain small patch of tall open woods that a few hunters have known and tended for years, although it is the least likely looking spot for game in the whole region. Yet if there is but a single woodcock in all Fairfield County, the chances are that he will be there. Several times after flushing a solitary woodcock in this spot I have gone over the whole place to find some reason for Whitooweek's strange fancy, but all in vain. The ground is open and stony, with hardly a fern or root or grass tuft to shelter even a woodcock, and there is absolutely no boring or sign of Whitooweek's feeding. From all external appearances it is the last spot where you would expect to find such a bird, yet here is where Whitooweek loves to lie during the day and to this spot he will return as long as there are any woodcocks left.

I have questioned old gunners about this spot—which I discovered by flushing two woodcocks at a time when none were to be found—and I find that it has been just so as long as they can remember. Years ago, when the birds were plentiful, five or six might be found here on a half acre at any time during the flight. If these were killed off, others took their places, and the supply seemed to be almost a constant quantity as long as there were birds enough in the surrounding coverts to draw upon. But why they haunt this spot more than others and why the vacant places are so quickly filled are two questions that no man can answer.

One hunter suggests to me, doubtfully, that possibly this may be accounted for by the migrating birds that are moving

southward during the flight and that drop into the best unoccupied places. The objection to this is that the birds migrate
by night, and by night this spot is always unoccupied. The
woodcocks use it for a resting place only by day, and by night
they scatter widely to the feeding grounds, where also the migrating birds first make their way. Whitooweek must feed
often, his food being easily digested, and he can probably make
no sustained flights; he seems to move southward by easy
stages, feeding as he goes. So the newcomers would meet the
birds that lately occupied the spot on the feeding grounds, if
indeed they met them at all, and from there would come with
them at daylight to the resting places they had selected. But
how do the newcomers, who come by night, learn that the favored spots are already engaged by day, or that some of the
birds that occupied them yesterday are now dead and their
places vacant?

The only possible explanation is either to say that it is a
matter of chance—which is no explanation at all—or to say
frankly that there is some definite understanding and communication among the birds as they flit to and fro in the night;
which is probably true, but obviously impossible to prove with
our present limited knowledge.

This fondness for certain spots shows itself in another way
when you are on the trail of the hermit. When flushed from a
favorite resting place, he makes a short flight up to the brush
tops and back again, and then goes quietly back to the spot
from which he rose as soon as you are gone away. He has also
the hare trick of returning in a circle to his starting point, and
occasionally, when you flush a bird and watch sharply, you
may see him slant down on silent wings behind you and light
almost at your heels. Once my dog started a woodcock and

remained stanchly pointing at the spot where he had been. I remained where I was, a few yards in the rear, and in a moment Whitooweek whirled in from behind and dropped silently into some brakes between me and the dog, not ten feet from the old setter's tail. The ruse succeeded perfectly, for as the scent faded away from the dog's nose he went forward and missed the bird that was watching him close behind. This curious habit may be simply the result of Whitooweek's fondness for certain places; or it may be that by night he carefully selects the spot where he can rest and hide during the day, and returns to it because he cannot find another as good while the sun dazzles his eyes. Or it may be a trick pure and simple to deceive the animal that disturbs him by lighting close behind, where neither dog nor man will ever think of looking for him.

When he finds good feeding grounds on his southern migrations, Whitooweek will stay with us, if undisturbed, until a sharp frost seals up his storehouse by making the ground too hard for his sensitive bill to penetrate. Then he slips away southward to the next open spring or alder run. On Shippan Point there is a little spring that rarely freezes and whose waters overflow and make a green spot even in midwinter. The point is well covered with houses now, but formerly it was good woodcock ground, and the little spring always welcomed a few of the birds. One Christmas time I found a woodcock there quite at home, within a stone's throw of two or three houses and with snow lying deep all around him. He had lingered there weeks after all other birds had gone, held either by old associations and memories of a time when only the woodcocks knew the place, or else, wounded and unable to fly, he had sought out the one spot in all the region where he might live and be fed until his wing should heal. Nature had cared for him tenderly, giving him food and a safe refuge at a time when all other feeding grounds were held fast in the grip of winter, but men, who can be kind and reasonable, saw no deep meaning in it all. The day after I found him a hunter passed that way and was proud of having killed the very last woodcock of the season.

There is one astonishing thing about Whitooweek which can scarcely be called a habit, but which is probably the discovery of one or two rare individuals more original than their fellows. Like the eider duck and the bear and the beaver, Whitooweek sometimes uses a rude kind of surgery for binding up his wounds.

Once while I was sitting quietly by a brook at the edge of the woods in Bridgewater, a woodcock suddenly fluttered out into the open and made his way to a spot on the bank where there was a light streak of sticky mud and clay. It was the early hunting season and gunners were abroad in the land, and my first impression was that this was a wounded bird that had made a long flight after being shot and that had now come out to the stream to drink or to bathe his wound. This may have been true or not, but the bird was acting strangely in broad daylight. I crept nearer until I could see him plainly on the other side of the little stream.

At first he took soft clay in his bill from the edge of the water and seemed to be smearing it on one leg near the knee. Then he fluttered away on one foot for a short distance and pulled tiny roots and fibers of grass, which he worked into the clay already smeared on his leg. Again he took more clay and plastered it over the fibers, putting on more and more until I could plainly see the enlargement. Thus he worked away with strange, silent intentness for fully fifteen minutes, while I watched and wondered, scarce believing my eyes. Then he stood perfectly still for a full hour under an overhanging sod, where the eye could with difficulty find him; his only motion was an occasional rubbing and smoothing of the clay bandage with his bill, until it hardened enough to suit him, when he fluttered away from the brook and disappeared in the thick woods.

I was sure that the woodcock had a broken leg and had deliberately put it into a clay cast to hold the broken bones in place until they should knit together again, but naturally I kept my own counsel, knowing that no one would believe in the theory. For years I questioned gunners closely, and found two who said that they had killed woodcocks whose legs had at one time been broken and had healed again. As far as they could remember, the leg had in each case healed perfectly straight instead of twisting out to one side, as a chicken's leg does when broken and allowed to knit of itself. I examined hundreds of woodcocks in the markets in different localities and found one whose leg had at one time been broken by a shot and then had healed perfectly. There were plain signs of dried mud at the break, but that was also true of the other leg near the foot, which only indicated that the bird had been feeding in soft places.

All this proved nothing to an outsider, and I kept quiet about what I had seen for a long time, until the confirmation came unexpectedly. Then a lawyer, well known all over my state, came to me and told me eagerly of a curious find he had made the previous autumn. He was gunning one day with a friend, and they shot a woodcock, which on being brought in by the dog was found to have a lump of hard clay on one of its legs.

Curious to know what it meant he chipped the clay off with his penknife and found a broken bone, which was then almost healed and as straight as ever. A few weeks later the bird, had he lived, would undoubtedly have taken off the cast himself, and there would have been nothing to indicate anything unusual about him.

So I give the observation now, at last, since proof is at hand, not to indicate a new or old habit of Whitooweek—for how far the strange knowledge is spread among the woodcocks and the wading birds no man can say—but simply to indicate how little we know of the inner life of the hermit, and indeed of all wild birds, and how much there is yet to be discovered when we shall lay aside the gun for the field glass and learn to interpret the wonderful life which goes on unseen all about us.